PERSPECTIVES & INFORMATION

This section explains what managed funds are, the different types available, how they operate, what investment managers do, what managed funds invest in, how different asset classes work, what fees you will pay, how managed funds achieve investment earnings and how they are taxed.

It also explains the multiple ways in which you can access managed funds, as well as the differences between buying them one by one or through a platform, which may be a wrap, managed account or superannuation fund, including a self-managed super fund.

Using this information, you will be able compare managed funds and choose one that best suits your needs.

Managed funds checklist

If you are looking to invest in a managed fund, this 10-point checklist should help you:

01 Does the managed fund have a proven track record of achieving competitive investment outcomes?

02 Have you read its latest information booklets, such as its product disclosure statement, prospectus and latest annual report, and have you visited its website?

03 Do you understand how the managed fund operates and are you comfortable with the organisations running it? Test yourself by explaining to a friend or relative how the managed fund works.

04 Do the annual investor statements make sense, are they easy to understand, and do they contain all the information you need to monitor your investments and total fees, and to handle your annual taxation reporting?

05 If you are accessing the managed fund through a platform, do you understand how this affects your managed fund, your fees and how you monitor your investments?

Remember: If you need advice on choosing a managed fund, you can always see a financial adviser (see page 63). To find a financial advice professional near you, please visit **www.selectadviser.com.au.**

06 How do the managed fund's investment returns stack up against similar managed funds and against other market and sector averages? For example, does it perform reasonably over the medium to longer term (three or five years) and does it manage its investment risks appropriately?

_____
_____
_____

07 What total fees will you pay each year, and are you confident that you are getting a reasonable deal? Remember that paying higher fees does not guarantee higher investment performance.

_____
_____
_____

08 Can you access your managed fund account online using the fund's website or using your mobile device?

_____
_____
_____

09 Does the managed fund offer extra features, benefits or services, such as special fee deals for family members or loyalty discounts for service providers it has strategic alliances with?

_____
_____
_____

10 Have you "road-tested" the managed fund's call centre by calling or emailing them or using their online chat to ask some questions? Did they respond, were they helpful, did they explain things in a way you could understand? If not, it's not a good sign.

_____
_____
_____

What are managed funds?

Managed funds are investment pools managed by investment experts. Investing through managed funds enables investors to combine their money into larger pools, which can enable them to take advantage of investment opportunities they may not otherwise be able to afford.

KEY POINTS

- Managed funds are investment pools run by investment experts.

- The responsible entity is the company that operates the managed fund, and it appoints the fund's investment manager.

When you make an investment you have two choices: manage the investment yourself as a direct investor or have someone else manage it for you. If you choose to have someone else manage your investment, the most popular way to do this is to place the money you want to invest into a managed fund.

The money you place in a managed fund is combined with money other people have placed in the same fund. This combined amount is used to buy the fund's assets (that is, make its investments). When an investor uses a managed fund they join forces with other investors, enabling them to participate in opportunities they may not be able to afford when acting on their own.

For example, through managed funds investors can invest in – or gain exposure to – specialist share market portfolios in Australia or overseas, commercial or industrial property, infrastructure projects, bond portfolios or other specialised projects.

Run by experts

The company that operates the managed fund is known as the **responsible entity**. If your managed fund is a listed investment company, the company board plays the role of the responsible entity and may not specify a separate responsible entity. It is their job to **administer** the fund, appoint the fund's investment manager (or selection of investment managers), monitor the fund's investments and market performance, and make sure the fund pays all its operating costs and tax bills.

The job of the **investment manager** is to ensure that the fund buys the best assets, which have the maximum likelihood of going up in value or making the most investment income, all while minimising the chances of something going wrong.

In most managed funds the investment manager is part of the same company group as the responsible entity – but not always. A good way to check your managed fund's credentials is to look at its offer documents and website. Good managed funds clearly explain which companies provide these services.

Getting your share

When you invest in a managed fund you are normally assigned units in the fund that are proportionate to the amount of money you have placed in it.

Most managed funds are set up as unit trusts, meaning the fund's responsible entity acts as the fund's trustee. It is responsible for ensuring the fund is properly managed and complies with all relevant laws.

For example, if you place $10,000 into a managed fund where the units are valued at $1 each, the fund manager may assign you 10,000 units from a total fund pool of 1 million units, meaning the fund has $1 million in total assets. If, over the next year, the fund's investments increase in value by 10% – so the total pool is worth $1.1 million – your 10,000 units will also increase in value by 10% to $11,000. Each unit would then be worth $1.10.

While most managed funds are unit trusts, a managed fund can also be set up under a company structure where the value of its investments is determined by how much they have increased in value and how much another investor wants to pay you for your share of the fund.

KEY POINT

- Most managed funds in Australia are unlisted unit trusts, and when you invest in a unit trust you are allocated units based on how much you place in the fund.

Managed funds are just a legal structure

Managed funds are formally known as "managed investment schemes". Despite this complex-sounding name, they are merely a legal or holding structure, in much the same way a company is a type of holding structure. Other holding structures include partnerships, family trusts, charitable trusts, super funds and sole traders.

Different types of managed funds

The different types of managed funds are based on how they are organised, what they invest in or how investors access them.

When you start researching managed funds you will come across terms such as retail managed funds, exchange traded funds, listed investment companies and model portfolios. Some are also categorised by whether or not they can accept superannuation contributions or by what they invest in. This chapter explains each of these categories.

Retail managed funds

These are managed funds available through mainstream investment managers, such as those associated with financial planning groups, banks, life insurance companies or other wealth management groups. In retail managed funds you buy units in the fund directly from the fund's responsible entity or through an intermediary that they have an association with, such as a financial adviser or stockbroker. Retail managed funds may also be referred to as public unit trusts or mutual funds.

Exchange traded funds

These are managed funds available on the Australian Securities Exchange (ASX). However, while units in exchange traded funds (ETF) are bought or sold through the ASX or other exchanges such as Cboe Australia, they are not listed on the exchange like a normal company share. Instead, you use the exchange's transaction system to buy or sell ETF units.

There are two main types of ETFs: indexed ones and actively managed ones. Indexed ETFs track a particular market index. For example, an ETF may track the Australian sharemarket index, the United States sharemarket index or the Australian government bond market index. An actively managed ETF is one where the investment manager tries to beat the market index and, unlike regular managed funds, it's available through the ASX and Cboe Australia.

When you buy units in these ETFs, even though you are using the exchange to make your transaction, the price of the units is determined by the price of the index tracked by the ETF, not by how much demand or supply there is for that particular ETF. ETFs managed this way

have very low fees because their investment manager only has to follow or mimic their market index. ETFs that are managed to beat a market index may be known as exchange traded managed funds (ETMF). There are a growing number of products that can be transacted both on an exchange or at a price determined by the manager based on its Net Asset Value when the exchange has closed for the day. These are called hybrid securities.

Listed investment companies

Listed investment companies (LIC) are a type of investment fund that is incorporated as a company listed on the ASX. Investors buy or sell shares in the company, just as they would buy or sell any other company shares. Like regular managed funds, LICs have an investment manager who is responsible for selecting and managing the company's investments. LICs do not need a responsible entity as the company board is responsible for how it is managed and administered.

LIC shares are traded on the ASX like regular company shares, which can result in the value of the LIC's share price reflecting not just the value of its underlying investments but how popular the LIC is. For example, a LIC may have very valuable investments in its portfolio– that is, have a high net tangible asset (NTA) value – but other investors might not trust the LIC's investment managers to perform in future, so the LIC's share price may be lower than its NTA. This is what market analysts mean when they say a LIC is "trading at a discount".

Model portfolios

Model portfolios are similar to regular retail managed funds. The difference is that in a retail managed fund, the investor buys units in the fund and investment decisions are made collectively by the investment manager on behalf of all the fund's investors. In a model portfolio, the investor owns or has "beneficial ownership" of the underlying investments.

Model portfolios may be designed around an investment theme, such as a particular segment of the sharemarket, for example, shares in large Australian or international companies or global real estate investment trusts (G-REITs). In a model portfolio the investment manager may assemble a portfolio that includes not just directly held company shares but also units in other managed funds like retail unit trusts, ETFs or LICs.

This more complex and flexible ownership arrangement means that the administrative systems used for model portfolios are much more sophisticated than those used by retail managed funds. These advanced administration systems are known as managed account platforms.

KEY POINTS

- There are four main types of managed funds: retail managed funds, exchange traded funds, listed investment companies and model portfolios.

- Superannuation managed funds are managed funds investors use for their superannuation.

- Regardless of what types of assets are held in a managed fund, they all have to follow the same rules and laws.

Superannuation managed funds

Superannuation managed funds are funds that hold superannuation savings, that is, retirement savings that attract concessional rates of taxation. The only difference between normal managed funds and superannuation managed funds is the rate of taxation that applies to investment deposits or investment earnings. There is no difference in the fund's investments, the role of the investment manager or what is expected of the responsible entity.

Asset classes and managed funds

An asset class is a group of common assets that have similar characteristics, for example, Australian shares, international commercial property or Australian government bonds. Sometimes people describe managed funds according to the asset classes they invest into, such as an Australian shares managed fund or a cash managed fund.

Managed funds have to follow the same rules and laws irrespective of what asset classes make up the assets owned by the fund. This means there is no difference between managed funds that hold investments in different asset classes, so it is a mistake to think these are different types of managed funds.

How to access managed funds

You can deposit money into a managed fund in a few different ways.

KEY POINTS

- Deposits into a managed fund can be made with an initial amount, as one-off extra payments or as regular deposits that are part of an investment or savings plan.

- You can transact with a managed fund directly, through your financial adviser or stockbroker, or through a platform.

- You can invest in managed funds through a super fund if it offers these as investment choices.

- If you have a self-managed super fund (SMSF) and you invest money from it into managed funds, the units or shares in the managed fund are held in the name of the SMSF rather than by you personally.

You transact with a managed fund when you deposit or place money into it or take money out. Putting money into a managed fund is sometimes called making a contribution. Taking money out is called making a withdrawal.

Deposits can be made with an initial amount, one-off extra payments or regular deposits that are part of an investment plan. You can withdraw all your money from a managed fund in one go, you can withdraw only part of it or you can arrange to receive regular payments in the form of what is known as an income stream.

When you place money into a managed fund, in practical terms what you are doing is buying units in the fund or buying shares in the listed investment company (LIC). When you withdraw money, what you are doing in practical terms is selling or redeeming units.

A managed fund might also pay you a distribution, which is when it makes a regular payment to you from its investment income. For example, a managed fund that holds investments in shares might make distribution payments to you from the dividend income it receives, or a managed fund that holds investments in property might make distribution payments from the rental income it receives.

When you transact with managed funds, the responsible entities of the funds have to follow special rules. These rules extend to intermediaries, like financial advisers and stockbrokers, which responsible entities may authorise to handle these transactions on their behalf.

These transactions can be made by cheque, in cash, or through EFT payments. To complete the transaction, investors have to fill in an application form, either on paper or online. They will then be issued with units in the managed funds. If they are buying shares in an LIC, the share transaction is handled in the same way as regular ASX share transactions.

In the sections below, we describe the people, agencies and authorised representatives you must use when conducting these transactions.

Transacting directly with the managed fund

Investors can transact directly with the managed fund of their choice. To do this, they must know the name, ID numbers and operator of the fund because they are approaching the fund directly.

Transacting through a financial adviser

Financial advisers are specially trained experts qualified to help investors establish and implement a financial plan. They are licensed by the financial consumer regulator, the Australian Securities and Investments Commission (ASIC), to act in your best interests and provide you with independent advice. This advice may include recommending particular managed funds to you. Financial advisers can be found at most banks, insurers and super funds or they are available through wealth management groups. A major advantage of using a financial adviser is that they have relationships with many managed fund

operators. They can provide you with a wide variety of choices when using administrative systems – known as platforms – that contain managed funds from across the market, spanning all the asset classes and investment types.

Transacting through a stockbroker

Stockbrokers are specially trained experts qualified to help you buy and sell market securities, such as shares and bonds, and many can also arrange managed funds transactions. While financial advisers specialise in providing advice, stockbrokers specialise in helping investors execute their securities market transactions. Stockbrokers can be licensed financial advisers, and financial advisers can be licensed stockbrokers.

Transacting directly through a platform

An investment platform is an administration system purpose-built to enable investors to handle their investment transactions with various types of managed funds, monitor their investment performance, administer their taxation liabilities and provide regular reports. Investment platforms may be referred to as investment wraps, portfolio services or managed accounts.

Financial advisers use platforms to offer a wide range of investment choices they make available to clients. Some of these platforms are now available to investors directly without having to go through an intermediary, such as an adviser or stockbroker.

Investors who transact with managed funds directly through investment platforms do not normally have the support of expert advisers. Therefore they are responsible for their own decisions.

Transacting through your super fund

Investors who are members of a super fund can use their fund's investment menu to make selections from a range of strategy and asset class options Most of these investment choices are managed and administered by the super fund itself, but some funds offer members extra choices that can include retail managed funds, exchange traded funds (ETFs), LICs and model portfolios.

When you transact with these options through your super fund, however, you have more restrictions because these investments are part of your superannuation. There are strict rules concerning how you access these investments due to the concessional taxation arrangements associated with superannuation and the requirement that these investments form part of your retirement savings.

Managed funds and SMSFs

If you have a self-managed super fund (SMSF) you can invest money that you have contributed into the SMSF into a managed fund. The managed fund units or shares are owned by the SMSF rather than by you, meaning they become assets of the SMSF.

In these cases, you are not accessing managed funds through the SMSF but using the SMSF's funds to invest into the managed fund. When you report the SMSF's assets you will include the managed fund units or shares alongside other assets of the SMSF.

Income from managed funds held in SMSFs is taxed at the nominal superannuation rate of 15% rather than at your personal marginal tax rates – this is why investing through an SMSF is so attractive for many investors.

IDPS, wraps and managed accounts

The administrative platforms investors use to access managed funds can be known variously as investor directed portfolio services (IDPS), wraps or managed accounts. These platforms are sophisticated gateways that enable your financial adviser or managed fund promoter to assemble many investment solutions in one place. IDPSs and wraps are essentially the same thing. Managed accounts are newer generation platforms that generally have more advanced features, such as being able to offer managed funds and model portfolios that let you own the underlying securities in your name rather than through the fund.

If you are investing for your superannuation, you will need to bundle these investments through your superannuation fund, which may be through a master trust or an SMSF.

Who runs your managed fund?

Managed funds use many expert advisers. Understanding the different roles they play will help you make better sense of how a fund operates.

KEY POINTS

- The people who run your managed fund are called responsible entities (RE).

- Investment managers look after your managed fund's investments.

- The RE may use asset consultants to help them choose which investment managers to use, and to help them decide their investment strategy.

- Specialist administration companies help responsible entities run the back-end administration of your managed fund, including its call centre.

Remember that a managed fund is an investment fund run by someone else who is an expert in managing investments. To understand how good your managed fund is, it will help if you first learn the main roles people play at a managed fund so you can properly judge each person based on their role and responsibility. To do this, you need to learn what these roles are and what they mean.

Responsible entity

The responsible entity (RE) is an Australian public company that plays the dual role of trustee and manager of the managed fund.

The RE is responsible for running the managed fund and appointing various service providers, such as investment managers, custodians, asset consultants and administrators.

The RE must act honestly, exercise all reasonable care and diligence, act only in the best interests of the managed fund's investors and treat all investors equally. REs are regulated by ASIC.

REs are not expected to be experts in all aspects of running a managed fund, but they are expected to know how to manage people who are. Your managed fund's RE is there to represent you, and make sure the fund is working properly for you and the other investors. If anything goes wrong with the fund, the buck always stops with them, and this motivates them to make sure that things are working properly.

Investment managers

The types of investments chosen by your managed fund or its RE will ultimately be vetted by expert companies that specialise in managing investments. These firms are called investment managers, though they can also be called fund managers or money managers. They are experts in various types of investments, and they are experienced in deciding if investments are worth making.

Investment managers decide what to buy (invest in) and when to sell or hold these investments to make the best return for the managed fund investors.

While investment managers look after the managed fund's investments, they do not operate the fund itself. This means if you have any queries, you should raise them with the RE. Taking these concerns to the investment managers will be fruitless, because investment managers are directly accountable to the RE, not the investors. Remember: the investment managers run the investments, the RE runs the fund. And even if the same company performs each role, they are separate responsibilities.

Asset consultants

When it comes to using investment managers, managed funds can choose from more than 900 investment managers in Australia, and from thousands available overseas. Not surprisingly, depending how managed funds are structured, the organisation running the fund may need help from special advisers who are experts in understanding investment managers and how to choose between them. These experts are called asset consultants or investment consultants.

Asset consultants help managed fund REs decide how much money they should invest into particular types of investments or asset classes, for example, how much money a fund should invest into overseas shares compared with Australian government bonds.

Some asset consultants have been so successful with their advising services that they have adapted these to create their own managed funds, which they now offer to investors. When this happens, asset consultants cross the line from being simply consultants to being fully fledged managed fund operators.

Administrators and platform providers

Responsible entities sometimes use specialist companies to help them administer their managed funds. These specialist administrators are experts in the government rules of operating a managed fund and in making sure the fund meets compliance and regulatory requirements.

Administrators make sure that every time an investor makes a deposit into, or a withdrawal from, a managed fund the transaction is recorded properly. Annual reports, member statements and government compliance reports are all produced and handled by your managed fund's administrators, who are directly responsible to the fund's RE. The administrator might also operate the managed fund's website, call centre and live chat function.

Administrators of managed funds are sometimes called platform providers, as they provide the back-end investment platform that makes up the managed fund in addition to providing regular administration services. Platform providers offer a mix of asset consultancy expertise to managed funds, and they are usually more sophisticated in their operations than regular managed fund administration companies.

Custodians

Many managed funds use special companies called custodians to hold their assets and to coordinate and keep track of the investment managers used by the managed fund.

Custodians act as an important check for managed funds because they help insulate the managed fund from fraud and dubious investment transactions. If your fund has a custodian in place, it means that if an investment fraud is perpetrated on the fund, the custodian would foot the bill, because a big part of their job is protecting the fund from fraud.

Most good managed funds use only very large and highly expert custodians. If your fund does not use a custodian that is separate from the managed fund (that is, it tries to handle this role itself) make sure you understand how the managed fund does this, because if it is not handled properly your investments could be at risk.

LICs and responsible entities

If you invest through a listed investment company, the company board also acts as the de facto RE.

Fees – how much and getting what you pay for

To understand how much you are really paying in managed fund fees, you have to demystify the different types of fees funds might charge you. The good news is that it is not as complex as it seems.

KEY POINTS

- The more fees you pay, the higher your investment returns must be to make up for them.

- While there are many types of fees, you can group them together to derive your overall total expense ratio.

- Paying higher fees does not get you better investment returns.

Your aim in selecting a managed fund is to find one that will make you as wealthy as possible by the time you withdraw your money, without exposing you to too much unnecessary investment risk along the way. To do this, your fund must earn consistently strong rates of investment returns – year in, year out.

Fees affect your investment returns

To give you a better chance of building your retirement savings, it helps if your managed fund charges reasonable fees. Why? Because what you get in your pocket is what's left from the investment returns after all the fees are taken out; it is no more complicated than that. So the higher the fees, the higher the returns have to be to leave you with more money in your pocket.

An example will highlight why this is so important to understand. If two investors achieve identical investment returns but one pays only 1% in fees each year while the other pays 2% in fees each year, then the member in the fund with the higher fee will have 10% less in their account after 10 years and 19% less after 20 years.

So paying higher fees can cost you big money. And this means if you are paying higher fees, you should make sure you use the managed fund shrewdly so that you more than make up the fees through better investment mixes that lead to higher investment returns.

All about the fees

There are six main types of managed fund fees you should know about:

- **Establishment fees**, also known as entry or upfront fees, may be paid when you set up your managed fund account.
- **Contribution fees** may be paid each time you make a deposit.
- **Management fees** are paid to your fund's responsible entity to manage the fund. This fee usually includes the fees paid to the investment managers. This fee is sometimes called the indirect cost ratio (ICR).
- **Performance fees** are bonus fees paid if the managed fund's investment performance is very high (for example, it exceeds its benchmark by, say, five percentage points).
- **Adviser service fees** may be paid to your financial adviser or broker each year for the advice and support they provide.
- **Buy/sell spreads** are transaction fees the investment manager may charge when you buy more units in the managed fund or redeem units.

These different fee types mean that the different people involved with your managed fund are getting a different share of your fees. For example, in many managed funds, the investment managers may only be receiving one-third of the total fees you are paying, which means there is no point blaming them for your high fees

Warning: Do not chase high returns by paying high fees because there is **no evidence** that paying higher fees buys better investment returns. Instead, research shows that paying higher fees usually only gets you more investment choices.

because they are rarely the cause of the problem.

A fee people love to hate is the contribution fee. This fee, if you are paying it, usually goes to your financial adviser or broker to cover the cost of talking to you and providing some basic financial advice. You can often get a discount on this fee if you ask for it or if you are contributing a large amount of money into your managed fund.

When a managed fund or a financial adviser or broker is willing to discount fees for you, this is sometimes called dialling down your fees. But if the fees dial down so much that the fund, adviser or broker don't believe they are being properly paid, then don't expect too much service from them. It's one of those balancing acts you have to navigate when choosing a managed fund.

Impact of managed fund fees over 20 years

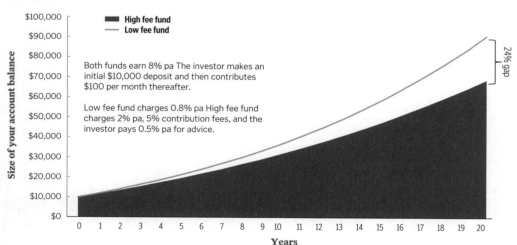

High fee fund
Low fee fund

Both funds earn 8% pa The investor makes an initial $10,000 deposit and then contributes $100 per month thereafter.

Low fee fund charges 0.8% pa High fee fund charges 2% pa, 5% contribution fees, and the investor pays 0.5% pa for advice.

Size of your account balance — Years

24% gap

Source: Rainmaker Information

The Good Investment Guide fee calculator
If you wish to compare managed fund fees, you should use *The Good Investment Guide* fee calculator, which converts all the fees you are paying into a single dollar amount.

It then applies that amount to your overall account balance to come up with your total fee as a percentage of your account balance. We call this percentage your total expense ratio or TER. Knowing the different fees charged by different managed funds means you can calculate the different TERs. It is important to realise, however, that a TER does not indicate the future performance of a managed fund – but we do know that higher fees rarely lead to better investment returns, and many of Australia's top-performing managed funds usually have low fees anyway. Why pay higher fees if you don't have to?

The TER calculator demonstrates that the biggest fee culprit is the management fee, because it is usually the highest, while the fees with least impact are usually the contribution fees. This is because

There are some tricks of the trade you should watch out for when it comes to fees and charges.

For example, beware of managed funds that try to confuse you by talking about fees charged to the fund and how they are different from fees charged directly to you. Anything that comes off the top of your investment return before you receive it is a fee to you – no ifs, no buts. Funds that do this aren't being dishonest, but they aren't being as transparent as they should be either.

To calculate your managed fund's TER, follow this example.

Step 1	What is your entry fee?	0.5%	
	Multiply this by your initial deposit. If you are depositing $10,000 this converts to 0.5% x $10,000 = $50.		$50
Step 2	What is your contribution fee?	2%	
	Multiply this by the extra contributions you made this year. If you are contributing $100 per month this converts to 2% x $1200 = $24.		$24
Step 3	What is your management fee?	0.35%	
	What is your indirect cost ratio?	0.45%	
	What performance fees do/did you pay?	0.10%	
	Add these figures together.	0.90%	
	Estimate your basic account balance: $10,000 - $50 + $1200 - $24 = $11,126 Add an estimate for your investment income: 5% x $11,126 = $556 Calculate your net account balance: $11,126 + $556 = $11,682 To estimate your management fees, multiply this by 0.90% to give $105.		$105
Step 4	Add all the dollar fees together.		$179
Step 5	**Calculate your TOTAL EXPENSE RATIO (TER) by dividing the total for Step 4 by your account balance: TER = 179 ÷ 11,682 = 1.53%**	1.53%	

Note that if you had nil entry and nil contribution fees your TER would be the 0.90% total described in Step 3, that is, it would reduce by nearly one-third.

contribution fees, while they sound nasty, apply to contributions and not the account balance. This means they are not a major problem unless you pay them when making a big initial deposit, such as transferring in a retirement lump sum.

If you want to receive a deal on your managed fund fees, you will get the best results if you dial down the management fees. It is, of course, good if you can dial down the other fees, too, but it's the management fees that you should worry about first.

While the average managed fund member across Australia pays a TER of about 1.5%, this covers everybody. This means that if you are in a managed fund charging less than 1%, you are in a very sharply priced fund. However, some very expensive funds can charge more than 2%. If you are paying high fees then you should be getting something very special, such as top-quality financial advice, a great range of extra features and lots of investment choices – and these features should be translating into higher returns.

What to expect from your managed fund

Your fund must describe the fees it charges in the product disclosure statement (PDS) in an easy-to-read table in the key features statement. This can usually be found towards the front of your investor booklet. Look for the section on fees and charges. If you don't have this booklet, check out your managed fund's website or call them and ask for a copy to be sent to you.

If your managed fund doesn't have a section in its PDS or website that describes all the fees, this is a red flag suggesting you should use another fund. The Commonwealth Treasury and ASIC have devised a template for funds to follow. It is compulsory for managed funds to use this template when describing their fees, so if a fund you are thinking about using isn't following these fee disclosure guidelines, then do not join. Poor fee disclosure is a very bad sign in a managed fund.

Also remember that your fund's rate of return described in your member statement is the figure left after all the fees are taken out (or it should be). If your rate of return is low, it may be that you are paying too much in fees. Conversely, just because fees are high doesn't necessarily mean your rate of investment return after fees is low either.

KEY POINTS

- Every extra 1% you pay in fees each year will cost you 10% of your potential investment over a 10-year period.

- The indirect cost ratio (ICR) is another term used to describe investment fees.

Indirect cost ratio

Some managed funds no longer declare investment fees and instead refer to indirect cost ratios (ICR). They use this term because these charges may not be paid directly by you to the managed fund, but indirectly because the investment manager's fee is deducted from the investment return before the unit price is calculated. For example, the investment manager may achieve a 10% investment return for the managed fund but their fee is 1%, so the net return applied to the managed fund is 9%. When you see an ICR, just think of it as another way to describe the embedded investment fee.

Deconstructing your managed fund fees

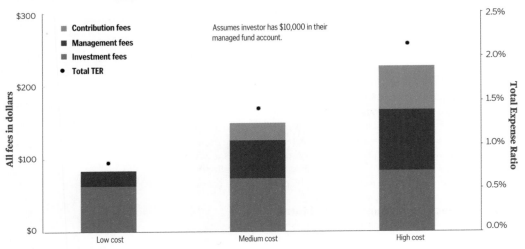

Source: Rainmaker Information

Managed fund fee types

Description	Applies to	Who gets it	What's normal	Negotiable
Establishment How much it costs to set up your account.	Initial deposit	Your financial adviser or broker	0 to 5%	Yes
Contribution How much it costs each time you contribute money into your managed fund.	Contributions	Your financial adviser or broker	0 to 5%	Yes
Management How much it costs to stay in the managed fund.	Account balance	The fund, but sometimes shared with the adviser	0.5% to 1.5%	Usually
Investment or indirect cost ratio How much you have to pay your investment manager.	Account balance	Investment manager	0.1% to 1.5%	Rarely
Performance Bonus fee paid to your investment manager if they do very well.	Account balance	Investment manager	0.1% to 0.5%	Rarely
Buy/sell spread How much it costs to enter or withdraw money from the managed fund. This is a form of contribution or exit fee.	Account balance	Fund and investment manager	Up to 0.30%	Rarely

Units and unit prices explained

Most managed funds are, in technical legal terms, unit trusts. When you invest into the managed fund you are really buying a share of the unit trust, meaning you are buying units in it.

The legal and tax structure of a managed investment scheme is typically that of a unit trust. The responsible entity of the unit trust is the legal owner of the assets that form the property of the trust, and the assets of the trust are beneficially owned by the investors in their capacity as unit holders. This structure ensures that the scheme assets owned by investors are quarantined from the fund manager operating the investment scheme (the legal term for what a managed fund is).

A managed investment scheme, once registered and established, may initially be seeded with money from institutional and wholesale investors or even the fund manager itself. Alternatively, it may simply raise money directly from the public, that is, retail investors.

The fund's rule book, known as its constitution, will dictate how much money the fund proposes to raise from investors and how many units in the fund are to be issued to investors. Each investor's ownership interest is reflected by the number of units in the unit trust (the managed fund) they hold. The size of the capital raising and the number of units to be issued will then determine the unit price, or vice versa.

For example, a fund manager may wish to launch an Australian Small Company Share Fund capped at $500 million. The terms of the fund constitution may stipulate that investors can subscribe to units at $1 per unit, in multiples of 1000 units. As a result, 500 million units will be up for issue. The unit price is simply the net asset value of the scheme assets, divided by the number of units issued to unit holders.

Alternatively, a managed fund may start out with a very small amount of money, perhaps $5 million, and increase in size over time by issuing further units to new investors. It may not have a cap on the amount of money it can raise from investors. Subsequent units will be issued based on a unit price that reflects the market value of those units at that time. Investors subscribe to units directly with the fund manager, i.e., they apply to buy them.

The greater the amount of money an investor deposits into the managed fund, the more units they are issued. Each unit holder has fixed rights in relation to the property or assets of the trust, such as rights to capital and income and voting rights as enshrined in the managed fund's constitution, as well as ordinary common law rights.

This system of unitisation enables a very large collection of assets to be divided among many investors in the most fair and equitable manner. It also enhances the marketability and liquidity of managed funds by facilitating efficient and timely exchange of the units, as incoming investors can apply for units, and exiting investors can simply redeem their units and hand them back to the managed fund in exchange for cash. In this way, it is very similar to the concept of a listed company issuing shares to shareholders.

The value of the unit price is usually recalculated at the close of trading every

KEY POINTS

- A managed fund is formally known as a managed investment scheme and is most often structured as a unit trust.

- When you deposit money into a managed fund or withdraw money from the fund you are really buying units or redeeming them.

- The rule book that defines how each managed fund operates is known as its constitution.

- The value of a managed fund's units is determined by the value of the fund's assets divided by the number of issued units.

- Investment income can be paid to unit holders in cash. This will reduce the assets in the managed fund and so reduce the unit price.

day, and performance of the fund can be tracked daily. Some managed funds that invest in property or real estate, which are less liquid assets, may be valued less often, for example, every month or every three months.

When you sell your units by redeeming them with the fund manager, the difference between the sell unit price and the original buy unit price represents a capital gain or loss for tax purposes.

Investment income is called a distribution

When a managed fund pays investors an income distribution (perhaps comprising dividends, interest or realised capital gains), the unit price will fall by the amount of the distribution per unit. This occurs because the net assets of the fund have been reduced by the size of the cash payment to investors. The unit price will fall once the units have gone ex-distribution, meaning that if you buy units after the relevant date you will not be entitled to receive the distribution until the next distribution period.

Some managed funds, such as unlisted property funds (which may be known as syndicates), have a different method for calculating distribution entitlements. Rather than being entitled to receive a distribution based on whether you held the units at a particular date, they will ascertain how many days each unit holder has held their units since the last ex-distribution date, and distribute income accordingly. If the income distributions are made every six months, but you acquired your units one month ago, you will only be paid one-sixth of a full distribution.

With this method, the unit price does not fall on the ex-distribution date by the amount of the distribution payable. This ensures an equitable distribution of income for all unit holders, but it is used only for a minority of managed funds.

This means that, in reality, managed funds have a three-way unit pricing system, because in addition to the fund's market unit price reflecting its net assets, the fund will also quote a buy unit price and a sell unit price. Typically, the sell unit price is about 0.10% lower than the market unit price, and the buy unit price is 0.10% higher than the market unit price – it is a buy/sell spread. This is designed to ensure transaction costs and brokerage incurred by the trust in purchasing or selling the underlying assets of the fund are equitably split between incoming and outgoing unit holders.

For example, a fund may incur brokerage and settlement costs of $500,000 in acquiring $500 million worth of shares for the fund on the ASX. Who should pay this brokerage? New unit holders buying into the fund or outgoing unit holders selling their units? The easiest and fairest method is to split the cost equally between unit holders who wish to buy into the fund, and those who wish to exit the fund.

How to work out your investment return

A managed fund might not tell you its annual investment return; rather, it will tell you its unit price. To convert this to an annual investment return, you simply subtract the unit price one year ago from the unit price today and divide this by last year's unit price. If there have been any distributions in the year these will have to be added onto the current unit price. To convert this to a percentage, multiply by 100.

For example, if your units today are valued at $1.20 and there was a distribution of $0.05 during the year compared to $1.10 one year ago, the difference is $1.25 - $1.10 which is $0.15. Convert this to a percentage by following this formula: ($0.15 ÷ $1.10) x 100 = 13.6%.

How your managed fund investments are taxed

While managed fund or unit trust income is not taxed, this doesn't mean it is tax free. To help you handle your tax affairs, your managed fund will provide you with all the information you need in your annual statement.

Managed funds do not pay tax, but that doesn't mean they are tax free. This is because the fund leaves it to each investor to manage their own taxation affairs. In this way, managed funds are tax agnostic because you pay tax on this income at your marginal tax rate.

To help you prepare the annual taxation statement that you must lodge with the Australian Taxation Office, your managed fund responsible entity will provide you with a detailed annual account statement. It will include a full listing of all the income and distributions you have received and describe how they apply to you.

Consolidated reporting

When a managed fund's responsible entity issues investors with a consolidated tax report at the end of each financial year, the report will show how much taxable income you, as the investor, need to declare, what your realised capital gains were, and what your unrealised (paper) capital gains were.

If you invested in a large portfolio of direct stocks, some of which were liquidated (sold) throughout the year, you would need to manually calculate the amounts yourself and develop your own consolidated summary for your annual taxation assessment. This can be done by your accountant – for a fee, of course – or if you are investing through a managed account platform it will be able to automatically generate this for you.

Managed funds may also allow you to check their information on the internet and track the performance of your investments as frequently as you wish, just as direct share investors can track their shares through online broking services. If you are invested in multiple markets across multiple asset classes, the ease of tracking performance through a fund manager is even greater.

KEY POINTS

- You must declare income you receive from your managed fund in your annual taxation assessment, so it can be taxed at your marginal tax rate.

- Franked dividends apply only to company income taxed in Australia and are available only to Australian resident investors.

- You may be entitled to a tax credit for tax paid overseas on your foreign investments.

You don't pay tax just because your investments increase in value

You only pay tax on income and distributions you receive from your managed fund. You do not pay tax on the notional gains of your managed fund units unless you redeem these units or this increase in unit value is converted into a dividend distribution payment.

The types of managed fund income distributions you may receive are:

Australian income

This is income paid on investments situated in Australia, whether in shares, units in a unit trust, bank deposits, property or other income-producing investments. It is income that an investor is entitled to in a financial year even though they may not have received it in that year.

Dividend income

Australian resident shareholders are tax-assessable on dividends paid out of any company profits, including capital profits and profits that are exempt from tax. Dividends include any distributions made by a company to its shareholders, including certain distributions made in a return of capital.

Dividends are included in the assessable income of a shareholder when they are paid, credited or distributed to the shareholder. Therefore, a dividend is taxable in the year the dividend cheque is posted to the shareholder even if the cheque is not received until the following year.

Franked dividend income

If your managed fund has received investment income from companies into which it has invested and these companies paid tax, the managed fund may be entitled to dividend imputation and franking credits. These are explained in detail in the section on Australian equities. Note that franked dividends can be paid only to Australian-resident individual shareholders or unit holders, and act to compensate them for being taxed twice on company profits income that has already been taxed.

There are some consequences that flow from receiving franked dividend income distributions:
- Both the dividend and the amount of the attached franking credit (reflecting tax paid by the company) must be included in the shareholder's or unit holder's assessable taxable income.
- The shareholder or unit holder is entitled to a franking offset equal to the franking credit.
- The offset can be applied against tax on any other income, but not against the Medicare levy. Any excess credits are refundable.

Where franked dividends are received through trusts and partnerships, the franking credits and corresponding franking rebates are generally apportioned between the beneficiaries or partners according to their share in the net income or loss of the partnership or the net income of the trust.

Imputation credit income

Imputation credits are itemised separately and included in taxable income. These are credits that investors receive if a company they invest in directly or indirectly through a managed fund has already paid tax on income from which they have received a distribution. These credits can be used to offset other tax liabilities.

Undistributed income

Generally, where some of the income is retained in the unit trust, the trustee is held responsible for tax on that amount, and the undistributed income in the unit trust is taxed at the top marginal rate. Such high tax rates apply to discourage investors hiding income inside trusts.

If the unit trust subsequently distributes these taxed profits, the beneficiaries are not liable for any further tax; but for capital gains tax purposes, the cost base is reduced by the amount of the distribution.

These general rules of thumb are subject to provisions in the fund constitution (for example, there may be a clause stating that the fund beneficiaries are entitled to all taxable income of the fund, whether distributed or not). The Tax Commissioner may impose penalties on managed fund responsible entities and their trustees where it is determined that trust income was not distributed to beneficiaries due to trustee negligence.

Capital gains income

The capital gain shown in a distribution statement consists of two types, each arising from different circumstances.

1. Capital gains that arise from the sale of assets within a fund, creating a net capital gain for the year, which must be distributed to investors. These capital gains are included in the income an investor has received and appear as taxable income.
2. Capital gains that arise if the investor makes a withdrawal from a fund. This is the amount that the fund manager estimates to be the capital gains tax liability on the sale of the units. The capital gain is listed under taxable income.

You do not pay capital gains tax just because your managed fund units have increased in value.

Foreign-sourced income

As a general rule, Australian tax residents pay tax on income from foreign sources, but how this works in practice can be affected by the operation of Australian double taxation agreements (DTA) with various countries. On top of this, Australia's tax legislation contains a range of tax concessions and exemptions for specific items of foreign-source income. Your managed fund will detail how these apply to you in your annual income distribution statement. If you have invested directly into an overseas-based managed fund, you will have to deal with the foreign-sourced income yourself when you declare your income on your annual tax assessment.

The way this works is that any time foreign income is derived by you, as an Australian resident, the gross amount must be included as assessable income, although a foreign income tax offset is allowed for any tax paid overseas. This foreign income, deductions and foreign tax paid must be converted to Australian dollars before you include them on your tax return.

These tax rules on foreign-sourced income apply to dividends, interest payments you have received, royalties, capital gains and pension payments.

Subject to any relevant DTA between Australia and the source country and subject to the source country's own domestic taxation laws, the foreign payer from where you received the income may withhold foreign tax from the payment made to you. In this case, the gross amount of the income, that is, before withholding tax, is treated as assessable income for Australian tax purposes. The amount of foreign tax withheld may be creditable against Australian tax liabilities.

Foreign-sourced capital gains are generally subject to Australian income tax under the capital gains tax (CGT) regime, subject to any relevant DTA. Note that some treaties that were negotiated before the current CGT measures were introduced may be silent or unclear regarding the allocation of taxing rights over capital gains.

Pensions and purchased annuities are generally assessable in the country of residence. Most comprehensive DTAs are structured in this manner; but a review of relevant treaty provisions is advisable.

Income paid to your financial adviser or broker

Any ongoing commission paid by an investment fund to an investment adviser in relation to an investor's investment in the fund is considered to be assessable income of the investor if the adviser is under an obligation to pass the commission onto the investor.

Distributions from trusts must, as a result, be included in the tax return of the year of entitlement, not necessarily the year of receipt.

Nevertheless, trusts are not normally taxed as long as all the net income of the trust (including any realised capital gains) is distributed to the unit holders (its beneficiaries). This applies to all unit trusts, including cash management trusts, mortgage trusts, equity trusts and property trusts.

History of managed funds in Australia

Australia's managed funds sector is less than a century old, yet it has grown into one of the most sophisticated markets in the world.

KEY POINTS

- Managed funds in Australia evolved out of the trust structures started by friendly societies.

- Australia's first modern investment unit trust started in 1936.

- Hooker Investment Corporation started Australia's first property fund in 1959.

- Hill Samuel, which would become Macquarie Bank, started in Australia in 1980.

- Bankers Trust's handling of the 1987 stockmarket crash popularised investment management.

Nineteenth-century Australia – before the introduction of publicly funded welfare, healthcare and education – was a tough place for families who weren't wealthy or didn't have high-paying jobs. To fill this void, member-based associations, such as friendly societies, formed to collect regular contributions from members and place them into common funds that would be used to support members in times of hardship.

Members of these societies held meetings in local halls, and while they were generally closed to the public, they were run democratically with elected office-bearers. As civic-minded groups, they would often run street parades to attract new members and support local causes.

Friendly societies were not investment institutions, but they laid the foundation for Australia's financial sector that would eventually comprise banks, insurance companies, investment managers, super funds and trust law. Some of Australia's most famous financial brands, such as IOOF, Foresters and Hibernian, have their origin in these groups. Even though the Australian Mutual Provident Society (AMP) started in 1849 and National Mutual Life Association of Australasia (National Mutual) started in 1869, these were not investment but insurance groups.

In those days, when working people wanted to save money their only option was depositing it into a bank. Wealthy people might have been able to place their money into a government-issued bond. In 1936, Hugh Walton changed all this when his company, Australian Fixed Trusts (AFT), launched a set of money market trusts through which members of the public, usually restricted to wealthier people, could invest in securities. AFT was based on investment trusts that had been operating in Britain since the 1870s. AFT's entry fees were 7.5% and promised returns of 10%pa.

The idea caught on. JBWere & Son, Australia's leading stockbroker (it had first opened in 1839), soon opened three similar money market unit trusts to supplement the equities investment trust they had been operating since 1928. Progress in the investment trust sector was nevertheless slow – by 1965 it managed only $250 million on behalf of about 100,000 people. In 1959, the Hooker Investment Corporation, which started life as a real estate agency in 1928, launched Australian Land Trusts, Australia's first unit trust specialising in property. It became popular and within a decade was offering 31 trusts.

Australia's 1960s stockmarket slump saw interest in investing through unit trusts wane, with many of the small equity trusts closing down. But in 1972 interest in unit trusts reawakened when the Trustees, Executors & Agency Company (TEA) expanded beyond just servicing the money market, with the help of Keith Halkerston, a senior executive at stockbroker Potter Partners. US investment banks soon followed in 1975, launching public managed funds focused on international equities. Sensing the trend, in 1980 UK merchant bank Hill Samuel opened in

Australia, launching a cash management trust. In 1985, following a series of acquisitions, the business obtained its Australian banking licence and renamed itself Macquarie Bank. The success of the newly formed Macquarie Bank prompted ANZ to buy AFT, Were Securities to launch a series of new funds, and Bank of America and the Royal Bank of Canada to enter the market. The momentum this was creating spurred several investment management specialists to launch their own retail funds, one famous group being Clayton Robard, which was started by former AFT executives.

Responding to this growing popularity of investment funds, magazine publishers in 1983 introduced Australia's first investment fund league tables, which triggered interest in assessing funds and sparked the launch of investment ratings and much broader public scrutiny of managed funds.

Up until the 1980s, the life insurance sector had largely ignored managed fund investments, preferring instead just to add a few investment features to their traditional policies. To catch up with the managed funds industry, particularly in the growing investment frenzy of the 1980s, the insurance sector began to respond with its own mergers and acquisitions. National Mutual merged with Temperance & General, establishing National Mutual Funds Management along the way. The Lend Lease property investment group acquired Mutual Life & Citizens (MLC), and the Dutch group ING acquired Mercantile Mutual.

The stockmarket boom also saw the launch of several big name investment management companies such as Portfolio Partners and Platinum, the launch of indexed equities investment funds, and the merger of several industry associations into the Investment & Financial Services Association, which was the forerunner of today's Financial Services Council.

The 1987 stockmarket crash brought this rapid development to a grinding halt, but it had a lasting positive effect – it popularised the value of quality investment management after it emerged that Australia's Bankers Trust group had successfully navigated the crash through the "put" options strategy they had championed. Another 1987 managed funds milestone was Sealcorp launching Australia's first investment platform. Eleven years later, in 1998, St.George Bank, now owned by Westpac, acquired Sealcorp, and in the following year Bankers Trust was acquired by Westpac.

Not to be outdone, the then recently privatised Commonwealth Bank in 2001 acquired the Colonial Mutual First State investment and insurance business and began assembling it into the group we today know as Colonial First State. Soon after, National Australia Bank acquired MLC, Westpac acquired Rothschild Funds Management, ANZ Bank launched its joint venture with ING and Merrill Lynch and Goldman Sachs acquired Potter Partners, all of which spurred some of the world's largest investment groups to enter the Australian market. The early 2000s would also see the launch of Australia's first exchange traded funds based on managed funds, first seen in Canada in 1989.

Since then Australia's managed funds sector has developed in tandem with the superannuation system to now oversee almost $4 trillion. It is the largest pool of investment capital the country has ever known.

Responsible entity reforms

In 1998, after a series of financial sector scandals, the government introduced the *Managed Investments Act 1998*, which restructured the managed funds industry to establish the single responsible entity (RE) regime that would make each scheme's operators fully responsible for them and accountable for all liabilities or losses. The Act took over from the prescribed dual-party investments system in which management of schemes was ambiguously shared by a fund manager and trustee.

The government's support for self-funded retirement, following the introduction of compulsory superannuation in 1992, reinforced the importance of the reforms. The need for the RE reforms was driven by a series of commercial property crashes at the end of the 1980s – in particular, the collapse of Estate Mortgage in 1990 and the Pyramid Building Society collapse in 1990, which led to massive losses for investors in retail investment funds.

1840

JBWere stockbroking opens in Melbourne.

1846

The Independent Order of Odd Fellows, which would become IOOF, opens in Melbourne.

1849

Australian Mutual Provident Society (AMP) opens.

1869

National Mutual Life Association of Australasia (National Mutual) opens.

1928

JBWere & Son launches Australia's first equities investment trust.

1980

Hill Samuel opens in Australia.

1975

US investment banks soon follow in 1975, launching equity oriented public managed funds.

1965

Australia's unit trust sector still managed only $250 million on behalf of around 100,000 people.

1959

Hooker Investment Corporation launches Australian Land Trusts, Australia's first unit trust specialising in property.

1936

Australian Fixed Trusts opens money market trusts in Sydney. JBWere & Son opens three similar trusts.

1982

Dutch group ING acquires Mercantile Mutual.

1983

First league tables comparing performance of investment trusts appear. National Mutual merges with Temperance & General, then establishes National Mutual Funds Management.

1985

Hill Samuel obtains a banking licence and rebrands as Macquarie Bank.

1987

Stockmarket collapses. Sealcorp launches Australia's first investment platform.

1998

St George Bank acquires Sealcorp. Responsible entity reforms introduced.

2022

Australia's managed investment market reaches $3.5 trillion.

2008

Westpac acquires St George Bank.

2000s

Australia's managed funds market begins evolving in tandem with Australia's modernised superannuation system.

2001

CommBank acquires Colonial Mutual First State. Exchange traded funds start in Australia.

What are asset classes?

When you invest, you are buying assets that you expect will either go up in value over time or deliver you income. These investments can be categorised into groups known as asset classes.

The main asset classes are company shares, property, bonds, cash or alternatives, which are more exotic or complex types of investments.

Shares are also known as equities because when you buy a share in a company you are buying an equity interest in that company. (Incidentally, this is why it's called a share in that company.) The value of the company shares you have invested in goes up or down depending on how profitable the company is and the price other investors are prepared to pay to buy those shares.

Property includes real estate, which spans office buildings, retail shopping centres and industrial estates such as factories, residential property or aged care developments. Property investments can be either the physical property (also called direct property) or shares in companies or units in funds that invest in or own property, for example, a LIC that specialises in property, or a managed fund that specialises in real estate investment, which is listed on the stockmarket – known as a real estate investment trust (REIT).

KEY POINTS

- The main asset classes are shares, property, bonds and cash.

- Assets that don't fit into these main groups are known as alternatives.

KEY POINTS

- Asset classes can be further categorised by the location of the asset, for example, Australian or overseas.

- Different asset classes have different investment return and risk characteristics.

Bonds are also known as fixed interest or fixed income because when you buy a bond you are really lending money to the entity – usually a government or company – that issued that bond. In return, the issuer agrees to pay you a fixed rate of interest over the term of the bond, which can be as short as 30 days or in perpetuity, when it has no maturity date. Sometimes the amount paid by the bond is based on a rate that varies over time, such as the cash rate. In this case the amount of the coupon will change when the underlying rate changes.

Cash can be physical in the form of notes and coins or overnight bank deposits. Its defining characteristic is that it doesn't lose capital value and is highly liquid. You have access to it pretty much any time you want.

Assets that don't fit neatly into these classes are known as alternative assets. They include more complex investments such as private equity, hedge funds and infrastructure.

Australian versus international assets

Asset classes can be further divided into other groups based on where the assets are located. This is why we refer to Australian equities, international equities and emerging markets equities, which are investments in companies in emerging growth economies, such as Brazil, Russia, India or China (a grouping known as the BRIC economies). Property can be classified in the same way.

Bonds can also be categorised according to whether the entity issuing the bond is based in Australia or in a major overseas country or emerging growth economy.

Risk and return characteristics

In addition to what assets may look like – that is, what they are physically – asset classes can also be defined according to their investment characteristics

Types of asset classes

Australian equities	Shares in companies listed on the Australian Securities Exchange (ASX).
International equities	Shares in companies listed on overseas securities exchanges, for example, the New York Stock Exchange, London Stock Exchange, Tokyo Stock Exchange.
Direct property	Physical or real property such as investments in land, buildings, commercial, industrial or retail shopping mall real estate.
Listed property	Shares in companies or funds that invest in property in Australia or overseas.
Australian fixed interest	Bonds issued by the Australian government or Australian-based companies, sometimes called debentures or credit securities.
International fixed interest	Bonds issued by foreign governments or overseas-based companies.
Cash	Actual cash such as term deposits or short-term highly liquid bonds.
Alternatives	*Private equity* – shares in private or small companies that are not yet listed on a securities exchange. This can include shares issued by tech start-ups. *Hedge funds* – special funds that, for example, trade options or derivatives. *Infrastructure* – investments into projects such as sea ports and airports, electricity and water utilities, telecommunications networks or hospitals.

such as their likely investment return, how risky they are, how fast they are expected to increase in value and how they distribute income.

Income from different asset classes can come in the form of dividends from shares, coupons from bonds (this is the technical term for a bond's interest rate payment), the yield from cash or rent from property. Income itself can be variable or stable. The income from shares comes in the form of a dividend payment that rises or falls depending on the underlying growth or decline of a company's profits. Income from bonds is generally stable for the life of the bond, but becomes variable (that is, may change) when the bond matures and the proceeds have to be reinvested.

The expected return from each asset class is determined by how risky it is. Investment risk comes in several forms: risk of losing money, known as capital loss; risk that income won't grow at a rate that matches inflation; or volatility risk, which is the extent to which the investment return fluctuates. These characteristics

play out differently for each asset class. For example, the price of equities can move around and sometimes goes through periods of significant capital losses. Nevertheless, over time you should expect equities to provide higher returns than fixed interest or cash.

On the other hand, the prices of fixed income securities are relatively stable. They are relatively stable because the prices do move, particularly when interest rates go through periods of dramatic increase or decrease, but not by as much as equity prices do.

By combining different asset classes, investors or their investment managers are able to trade-off or counterbalance these returns and risk characteristics. For example, they may put equities and fixed income into the same portfolio because while their investment value (asset price) may change, they tend to move in opposite directions, meaning they insulate each other in case, say, equities have a bad year and lose value. This loss can be offset by the investment performance of the bonds.

What is a hedge fund?

Hedge funds are special managed funds that don't focus on investing in particular types of physical assets but on exploiting investment processes such as trading options or derivatives. They may also invest money they have borrowed with the expectation that they will repay the loan quickly with their investment profits, or they arbitrage across markets. Hedge funds can achieve very high investment returns, but this comes with high risks and they are therefore suitable only for investors who understand these risks.

What is diversification?

Diversification is when you mix different asset classes into your portfolio to manage your investment risk.

KEY POINTS

- Different asset classes have different expected investment returns and risks.

- Using these characteristics, managed fund portfolio managers can design their portfolio with very specific investment return expectations and risk features.

- Growth assets include equities and property.

- Defensive assets include fixed interest and cash.

Diversification is one of the most overused and least understood concepts in investing. At its most simple, diversification is about creating a portfolio of different asset classes in order to reduce the overall investment risk of the portfolio while still maximising the chance of achieving reasonable investment returns over the medium and longer term.

The principle behind diversification is that different asset classes have different expected investment returns over the medium and longer term, offset by different expected investment risks. By mixing asset classes together, investors, or a managed fund's investment manager, are able to assemble a portfolio that they believe will suit likely future economic conditions.

For example, over the longer term, equities achieve higher average returns, but this comes with high levels of

investment risk, while fixed income assets achieve lower long-term average returns, but with lower investment risk. Property achieves long-term returns midway between equities and fixed income, with mid-range investment risk. Cash, on the other hand, will achieve low long-term returns, but comes with very low or even negligible investment risk.

By mixing equities, property, fixed-income bonds and cash into one portfolio, in years when equities and property perform strongly the overall portfolio will still perform reasonably well, but in years when they underperform the returns are offset by the more stable performance of the fixed-income assets and cash.

Diversification is improved when asset classes and the specific securities the managed fund invests into do not move in the same direction at the same time, for example when equities go down in value, fixed income assets should still go up in value. By combining assets with different performance behaviours, investors are able to achieve their goals with a smoother ride because the overall portfolio has lower investment risk.

By mixing asset classes in certain proportions a managed fund's investment managers are able to design their portfolio with particular investment return and risk expectations to suit the risk appetite or tolerance of their investors. This can be achieved to quite a precise level of likelihood by adding or subtracting specific asset classes in pre-determined proportions.

These expected investment returns and risks are shown in the graph below and the table on page 32.

Different asset classes suit different economic conditions

Another way to view portfolio diversification is that each asset class thrives in different financial and economic environments. As the environment changes different asset classes perform better or worse.

The following is a brief example of how this works. Say the economy is going through a strong and sustained period of growth due to low interest rates, that is, it is very cheap to borrow money. This growth allows companies to raise prices, increase sales

and make higher profits. This leads to higher prices for their shares.

Companies start competing for office space as they make more things, hire more people, and sell more goods. The increased demand for property means landlords can raise their rents, making their properties more valuable. Cash and fixed income, however, have low returns due to the low interest rates.

Later on, the central bank becomes concerned about rising inflation because of higher wages and higher prices. It tries to cool the economy by increasing interest rates. Cash becomes more attractive. Initially, fixed interest might have negative returns as yields rise and the value of existing bonds decreases. As the prospect for future profits reduces, share prices fall. As interest rates hit a peak, bonds become more attractive. Later, when interest rates fall, bond prices rise.

This illustrates how asset classes behave in different ways as the economy moves through different cycles. Since it can be difficult to predict asset prices in the short term, holding a diversified portfolio of assets remains the best way of smoothing returns over any time period. All countries go through these economic cycles and most asset classes have periods of negative returns.

Investment returns in each major asset class – December 2021

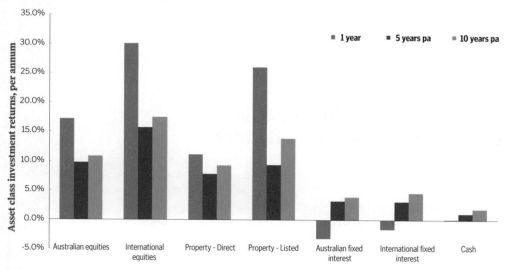

Source: FactSet, Rainmaker Information

What are growth and defensive assets?

Growth assets	Defensive assets
Growth assets are those that are expected to grow in value over time. The reason their value grows is that the income they produce (usually in the form of profits and dividends) also grows. Investors know that an asset that produces a growing income is worth more to them than an asset that produces an income that doesn't change.	Defensive assets, also called income assets, are those that are expected to hold their value regardless of economic conditions and deliver investment income. For this reason, they play a protective role in investment portfolios, particularly as a hedge against inflation. As a result, they are considered to be more conservative or moderate in style than growth assets.
The downside is that growth assets have more investment risks, that is, their value can fluctuate or even go down.	Defensive assets have lower investment risk than growth assets, that is, they have a very low risk of losing value. However, they are expected to achieve much lower long-term rates of investment return than growth assets.
Asset classes with these characteristics include equities, property and some alternatives like private equity and some hedge funds.	Assets with these characteristics include bonds, cash and infrastructure.

Asset classes and their expected investment returns and risks as at December 2021

		Div/ yield pa	Retained earnings pa	Growth pa	Franking credits pa	Total expected return pa	Volatility pa	Probability of negative return over one year
Growth assets	Australian equities	4.0%	2.0%	2.0%	1.0%	9.0%	15%	27%
	International equities	2.0%	4.0%	3.0%		9.0%	15%	27%
	Property - direct	5.0%		1.0%		6.0%	6%	16%
	Property - listed	5.0%		1.0%		6.0%	10%	27%
Defensive assets	Australian fixed interest	1.5%				1.5%	3%	25%
	International fixed interest	1.5%				1.5%	3%	25%
	Cash	1.0%				1.0%	0%	0%

Source: Rainmaker Information

What's your investment strategy: growth, balanced or moderate?

When you compare managed funds that use diversified investment strategies you will come across terms like "growth", "balanced" and "moderate". These are words managed funds use to categorise how highly weighted they are to growth assets, such as equities and property, or how weighted they are to defensive assets, such as fixed interest or cash.

- Growth managed funds have between 75% and 100% of their portfolio in growth assets.
- Balanced managed funds have between 55% and 75% of their portfolio in growth assets.
- Moderate managed funds have between 35% and 55% of their portfolio in growth assets.
- Conservative managed funds have less than 35% of their portfolio in growth assets.

Australian equities

Australian shares are the most popular asset class for investors thanks to privatisations and the power of dividend imputation and franking credits.

Australian equities are shares in companies listed on the ASX. These companies, for the most part, do most of their business in Australia, although many also earn income from international operations.

Shares represent part ownership of a company and give their owner a share of the company's profits, which is the portion left over after deducting the cost of running the business, the cost of its debts and the payment of corporate tax.

The value of Australian shares available on the ASX as at December 2021. amounted to a staggering $2.6 trillion, which is bigger than the value of the entire Australian economy.

The ease with which investors can trade shares on the ASX and the large volume of company shares available helps explain why Australian equities are Australia's largest investor asset class. But this popularity is also significantly boosted by taxation concessions available to investors, known as dividend imputation and franking credits.

KEY POINTS

- Australia's sharemarket is valued at almost $2 trillion.

- Investors make money from shares in two ways: from the change in the price of shares and from dividend payments.

KEY POINTS

- Dividend payments are concessionally taxed by a system known as dividend imputation and franking credits.

- Franking credits are special notional payments investors receive to compensate them for the tax already paid by companies before paying out dividends on which investors have to pay personal income tax.

Australia's sharemarket

Australia's sharemarket consists of 11 major sectors that reflect the activities of companies available on the ASX: financials, materials, healthcare, industrials, consumer discretionary, real estate, consumer staples, energy, information technology, telecommunication services and utilities.

The largest sector is financials – this includes the banking sector – which makes up 29% of the ASX market value, followed by the materials sector, which makes up 19% – this includes commodities-based manufacturers like steel makers and miners. Healthcare makes up 11%, with consumer staples at 5%, industrials 7% and real estate 7%. These six leading sectors comprise almost 80% of Australia's sharemarket.

Dividend imputation and franking credits

To encourage people to invest in Australian shares, in 1987 then prime minister Bob Hawke and treasurer Paul Keating introduced a taxation concession system that allowed Australian investors, when calculating the taxation liability on their Australian share investment earnings paid as dividends, to take into account the tax that companies have already paid on their profits. In practical terms this means investors only have to pay the difference between the lower company tax rate and their marginal personal income tax rate.

For example, if an investor is liable to pay a 45% marginal personal taxation rate and the companies in their Australian shares portfolio paid an average 30% tax rate on their profits, then the investor would only have to pay 15% tax on the dividends they received from these Australian company shares.

Meanwhile, a self-managed super fund that is liable to pay tax at only 15% would receive a 15% tax credit, because while their Australian company share earnings have already been taxed at 30% their SMSF tax rate is 15% lower.

ASX share market segments – 2021

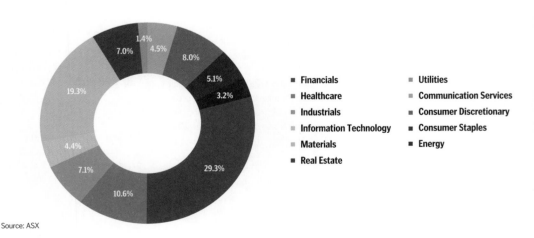

Source: ASX

To perform this adjustment – taking into account the tax already paid on company profits from which the dividend payments were made – companies gross up their dividends by a notional amount known as a franking credit.

Franking credits are available only to Australian investors. They ensure that dividends from Australian company shares are not taxed twice, that is, the investor does not pay personal income tax on Australian company dividends paid from profits that have already been taxed. Dividend imputation and

franking credits can reduce the amount of tax paid by Australian investors and may result in a tax credit where the Australian Tax Office gives the investor a refund.

If an Australian company pays tax to foreign governments on the portion of its profits earned overseas, this diminishes the amount of overall profits subject to Australian tax, which leads to a reduction in the franking credit available to Australian investors. This reduced franking credit is known as a partial franking credit.

ASX segment breakdown in more detail – December 2021

ASX segment	% of ASX	Investment return		Largest companies in segment
		1 year	5 years pa	
Financials	29%	-6.3%	1.6%	Commonwealth Bank
Materials	19%	18.2%	21.9%	BHP
Healthcare	11%	4.1%	18.1%	CSL
Industrials	7%	11.3%	11.6%	Transurban
Real Estate	7%	-0.3%	6.5%	Goodman Group
Consumer Discretionary	8%	-4.6%	7.0%	Wesfarmers
Consumer Staples	5%	6.2%	11.1%	Woolworths
Energy	3%	57.8%	24.4%	Woodside Petroleum
Communication Services	4%	4.6%	-4.4%	Telstra
Information Technology	4%	-27.6%	3.0%	Computershare
Utilities	1%	-16.7%	3.6%	APA Group

Source: ASX, Rainmaker Information

How you make money from Australian shares

There are two main ways investors make money from owning shares in Australian companies:

1. Change in valuation of the share price – if the company is worth more now compared to when you bought your shares, the difference represents how much money you have made from owning those shares.

2. Dividends paid, company earnings or net profit – when companies earn profits, some of this is paid out to shareholders in the form of dividends. The rest is retained by the company in order to help fund future growth, which can increase the value of the shares.

International equities

Australian company shares make up approximately 2% of all company shares available around the world, so investors should consider investing in international companies to access global opportunities.

Australian companies represent only about 2% of all company shares available around the world, yet the average Australian managed fund has around the same proportion of its investments in Australian equities as it does in international equities. Investors who manage their own assets, however – such as many with self-managed super funds – tend to have a higher weighting to Australian shares and much less invested internationally.

While there are some benefits to Australian equities – higher dividends and franking credits, for example – they do not have the same exposure to major world industries as international equities.

International company sectors

Fifty-nine per cent of the Australian market is dominated by financial companies (think the big four banks), materials companies such as BHP, and healthcare companies such as CSL Ltd. Only 8% is in the telecommunications and the information technology sectors. International markets, however, have much greater exposure to high-growth sectors like technology (think Apple, Alphabet – the company that owns Google – and the China-based digital media giant Ali Baba), automotives and pharmaceuticals. Investors who want a truly diversified portfolio should include these sectors or they risk missing out on being exposed to some of the world's fastest-growing companies.

Country segments

Investment in international equities can also be made based on where the companies are located, for example, in developed markets like the US, Europe, Japan or Australia, or emerging markets like China, India, Eastern Europe and South America.

Developed markets represent countries with advanced economies and capital markets. Emerging markets have lower economic development, but often these economies are growing rapidly. Emerging markets represent significant investment opportunities, which are offset by less liquidity and transparency regarding how companies operate, and lower standards of governance (how they are regulated).

While developed economy equities markets represent 88% of the global sharemarket, the emerging market share is still five times the size of Australia's 2% share of the global sharemarket.

How managed funds make money from international shares

Just like with Australian shares, there are two main sources of return for international shares. The first is company earnings or net profit. Some of this is paid out in the form of dividends to shareholders while the rest is retained by the company in order to help fund future growth. The second is the change in valuation or price of the company. This is what the market thinks the company is worth based on the price they are willing to trade its shares for each day. The income you receive is made up of dividends from the underlying shares and realised capital gains from selling shares that have gone up in price.

KEY POINTS

- Australia's sharemarket is heavily focused on financial, resources and healthcare companies.

- Investors who want exposure to high-growth industries like technology or digital media should consider investing in international companies.

- When you invest internationally you won't receive franking credits.

World sharemarket compared to Australia – 2021

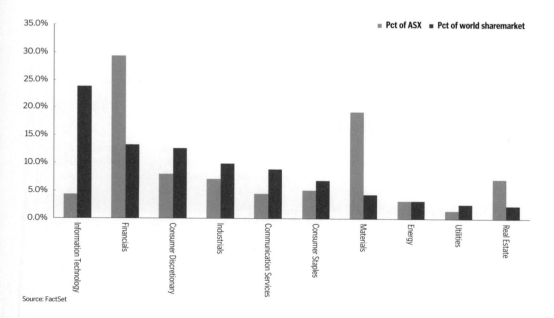

Source: FactSet

The sheer size of the international equities asset class means there is a fund to suit every investor – whether they want a fund for the long term or they have a particular investment view they want reflected in their portfolio.

The most general form is a fund that covers the developed world. The next most common form is what is called an "all countries" fund. This includes both developed markets and emerging markets. Next are pure emerging markets funds. These can cover all emerging markets or just certain geographic regions (usually Asia outside of Japan) and single countries such as India or China.

Managed funds can also be focused just on specific countries or regions, such as the US, Europe and Japan.

There are also sector and theme funds. These cover different industry sectors, such as healthcare or technology, or worldwide themes the manager thinks will benefit specifically from global trends (such as an ageing population or the growing middle class in emerging markets).

International equities funds come in all shapes and sizes

Geography	Sectors/themes	Market capitalisation	Performance objectives
Developed world	Industry sectors	Large companies	Match the index
All countries	Yield	Small companies	Beat the index
Emerging markets	Global trends		Downside protection
Regional			

To hedge the Australian dollar or not

Investment in international shares can be made on a currency-hedged or currency-unhedged basis. When the investment is made on a currency-**hedged** basis the returns from international shares are not affected by changes in the relative exchange rates of the Australian dollar and the home currencies of the international shares.

When the investment is made on a currency-**unhedged** basis the return from the investment is affected by any change in the value between the Australian dollar and the international currency. For example, when the Australian dollar rises (appreciates) against the international currency, the returns to the Australian investor are lower than they would be for the local international investor.

International shares are considered high risk because of the potential for loss of capital. This is more likely over short time periods rather than long time periods.

Property

Property is all around us in the form of office buildings, factories, retail outlets, hospitals and farms. It is an attractive asset class because it has both growth and income characteristics.

Managed funds invest into property in one of two ways. They buy real property assets, known as direct property, or they buy shares in investment companies or units in other funds that own direct property. Either way, the underlying assets are the same asset class and should exhibit the same investment returns and risk characteristics. The total value of these listed and unlisted property trusts in Australia is around $250 billion.

The main types of property for investment purposes are:

- Offices – medium-to-large-scale office buildings in and around regional centres and major cities.
- Industrial properties – warehouses, factories, storage facilities and industrial parks.
- Hotel and leisure properties – hotels, cinemas and theme parks.
- Retail properties – shopping centres, shopping malls and large stand-alone outlets.

Property trusts

While many Australians invest directly into the property market by holding residential property for rent, it is easier, cheaper, more liquid and geographically diverse to invest through a managed investment trust. These trusts are usually listed on the ASX and are called real estate investment trusts (REITs).

Investors can also buy units in property investment trusts that are not listed on the ASX. These are called unlisted trusts.

Both REITs and unlisted trusts hold direct property. It's just that the trust itself may be listed – this distinction can be ambiguous because unlisted property can sometimes also be called direct property even though the investors are buying units in the trust rather than being direct owners of the commercial property inside the trust.

There are 20 A-REITs listed in the S&P/ASX 200, with a market capitalisation of around $150 billion. This represents around 7% of the value of the S&P/ASX 200 at December 2021. To put this in perspective, the top four Australian banks represent around 16% of the Australian sharemarket, meaning AREITs represent only about one half the valuation of the banking sector.

A-REITs can be one of the higher-returning sectors of the stockmarket, although they are subject to periodic volatility in their capital values. They are one of the highest-yielding investment sectors available, explaining why property trusts are so popular. This is on top of their capital appreciation, which is determined by the traded price of the units in these REITs on the ASX. Expected capital growth of property is less than investors expect for listed equities because less of the trust's income is retained for reinvestment.

A-REITs pay out at least 100% of their entire taxable income to unit holders. This means they do not have to pay tax themselves. Some REITs pay out more

KEY POINTS

- The property investment market is separated into property that is directly held by the investor and property that is held through trusts.

- The main property segments are industrial, offices, hotels and leisure, and retail.

- Property has some of the highest yields available in the investment market.

than 100% of their taxable income as their cashflow often exceeds their taxable income due to deductions for depreciation and building expenses. Distributions can take the form of regular income or tax-deferred income, where the value of the distribution is deducted from the initial capital cost of the investment.

It is also possible to invest in international or global REITs through managed funds specialists in the property asset class – these may be referred to by their acronyms I-REITs or G-REITs.

Unlisted and hybrid property trusts

Unlisted trusts directly own a portfolio of real estate assets and are not listed on the ASX. Many hold capital raisings before they purchase portfolios and only expect to exist for a limited time before returning capital (and profits) to investors. Others exist in perpetuity. The costs of buying into and selling out of unlisted trusts is much higher than for funds that invest in REITs. This ensures that investors tend to stay invested in unlisted property trusts for longer. Unlisted funds may also change the terms of applications and redemptions to ensure that properties are not sold at inopportune times just to meet redemption requests.

There is also a hybrid form of trust that invests in both listed property trusts and direct property. These funds have some of the liquidity associated with REIT funds with the benefits of owning and managing properties directly.

Returns from unlisted trusts come from yield and changes in their capital valuation. One of the key differences between listed and unlisted trusts is that the price of unlisted trusts is determined by property experts who conduct periodic valuations of all the trust's assets, whereas the valuation of a REIT is determined by the price other investors on the ASX are prepared to pay for shares in the REIT. This is one of the reasons why unlisted trusts can have less volatile returns than REITs.

Making money from property funds

The main way managed funds make money from investing in property is by earning rental income. They should also make capital gains as the property increases in value either through the forces of supply and demand or through building upgrades.

This means a managed fund's investment returns from property comes in two parts: from income and capital growth. Think of this as similar to how

What determines a property's value?

The value of the property is determined by the current rental yield and the potential for increasing rents in the future. This includes the types of amenities on offer, location, how new the building is or how long it has been since the last refurbishment. It will include the composition of tenants. Single tenants with long leases may be attractive, while short remaining leases may mean that the property may have trouble attracting new tenants.

Returns from property are tied up with the supply of similar properties and overall demand in the economy. Oversupply forces rents and property values lower. Due to the cost and time of obtaining land, securing permits and building property, a booming economy may create demand that cannot be met with the existing supply, thus leading to higher prices.

Property's investment characteristics

These factors lead to property having unique characteristics that make it different from other asset classes. It is specific to a location, requires maintenance to ensure its continuing usefulness to tenants, is illiquid (meaning it can take a long time to buy or sell), and is subject to high transaction costs. As a result, property is considered to have a moderate level of risk, that is, lower investment risk than equities but higher risk than fixed-interest bonds.

managed funds make money from investing in equities: from company dividends as well as from the increase in share prices.

In this way, rental income is similar to interest payments on a bond or fixed-interest investment, for example, a bank term deposit. Both are calculated as a yield (percentage return) on the capital value at the time the lease was signed or the bond was

issued. When a property tenant takes out a lease they do so for a certain period of time and pay rent based on a formula that may include allowances for rent increases due to factors such as inflation or their business turnover.

Yields and capital returns available from different segments of the property market are detailed in the table below.

ASX REIT sectors and their yields – 2021

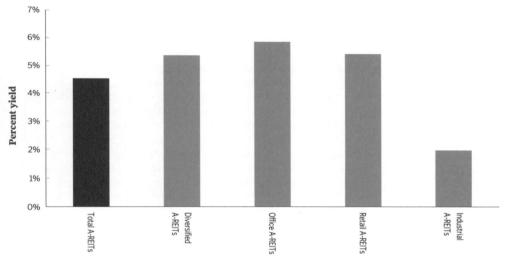

Source: FactSet and Rainmaker Information

Overview of S&P/ASX 200 Australian REIT sector at December 2021

	Value	Number of REITs	12-month yield	12-month capital return	12-month total return
S&P/ASX 200 / A-REIT	$148,613	21	4.5%	21.6%	26.1%
S&P/ASX 200 / Diversified A-REIT	$49,562	8	5.4%	16.3%	21.7%
S&P/ASX 200 / Office A-REIT	$13,190	2	5.9%	15.8%	21.6%
S&P/ASX 200 / Retail A-REIT	$33,403	7	5.4%	9.7%	15.2%
S&P/ASX 200 / Industrial A-REIT	$47,306	2	2.0%	39.9%	41.9%

Source: FactSet, Rainmaker Information

Fixed income bonds

Fixed income and bonds are the world's biggest asset class. Understanding how they work will help you see how they can fit into your managed funds portfolio.

KEY POINTS

- Bonds are loans made by investors to governments or companies that need capital.

- The bond market is the world's biggest asset class.

- Before investing in a bond you should know who issued it, its credit quality and its duration.

- Managed funds make money from their bond portfolio through aggregate interest rate payments and changes in the capital values of the bonds in the portfolio.

Bonds and fixed income assets are the biggest investment asset class in the world. At an estimated $US226 trillion in 2020 as the world was hit by a global health crisis and global recession, this makes them around three times the size of world equity markets.

While bonds sound complicated, they are just loans – when you invest in bonds you are agreeing to lend money to someone who needs it, whether they are a government, a business or a consumer. But unlike normal loans where most people go to their bank and ask to borrow money, with bonds the group that wants to borrow the money goes to the investment market to issue a contract, which is really just a request for how much they would like to borrow, the interest rate they are willing to pay and the term, that is, how long they want to pay off the loan. Often loans are auctioned, where the investors offering to receive, or accept, the lowest yield get to buy the bond on offer.

The interest rate, which makes up the yield on the investment, is called the coupon rate, and the term of the loan is referred to as its period until maturity.

In practical terms this means that when a government or a company issues a bond they are simply borrowing money, and when an investor such as a managed fund invests in that bond they are simply agreeing to lend money according to the conditions of the bond. This is why bond markets are also called the debt markets.

The bond market is made up of several segments based on who issues the bond, its quality or level of risk and how long until it matures. Investors should be aware that their managers make money from bonds through both the yield and changes in the bond's capital value.

Government bonds

The largest sector of the bond market by size are bonds issued by governments. For example, if the Australian government runs a budget deficit – meaning its annual taxation receipts are less than its annual income – because it doesn't have that money in taxation receipts, it has to borrow it. While governments could just go to the bank to borrow the money, because they are so big it's cheaper for them to go directly to large-scale investors and get lower rates of interest than a bank would charge.

Investors like lending money to governments because governments, in theory, can just increase taxation rates if they need money (despite the risk that this can lead to a currency crisis). As a result, governments should never run out of money to repay their debts – this makes them low-risk borrowers and highly favoured by investors. And because governments are so often running up bigger and bigger debts it means there is never a shortage of governments issuing new bonds. This makes government bond markets highly liquid.

Governments being at very low risk of not repaying their bond debts is referred to as them having a very low chance of defaulting on this debt. But some governments have gone through periods where they have not been able to repay bond investors. Recent examples are Turkey in the 1970s, Russia in 1998, Argentina in 2001 and Greece in 2012. Even the US and UK have defaulted on their debts at certain points in their history.

While governments having huge debts is a problem, it's actually a bigger problem for the investors who loaned them the money because if the country's economy collapses the bond investors won't be paid. This means that even though the US is the world's biggest borrower, it's also crucial for everyone to help the US economy recover quickly and perform as strongly as possible.

Largest government bond markets June 2021

Country	$A billion
United States	34,277
Japan	13,919
China	10,859
United Kingdom	4,984
France	4,008
Italy	3,769
Germany	3,265
Canada	2,645
Spain	2,056
Australia	1,377

Source: Bank for International Settlements

Private sector bonds

The second largest sector is private sector bonds, referred to as corporate debt. Some large companies are bigger than countries in terms of their balance sheets and revenues, and they issue debt of the highest quality. For example, in the US, AT&T is known as the most indebted company in the world with outstanding bonds of around $US147 billion. The global corporate debt market is estimated to be worth around $US8 trillion, or $11 trillion in Australian dollars.

The corporate bond market in Australia, in contrast, is estimated at around $600 billion, meaning it's only about 60% the size of Australia's government bond market.

It may also surprise investors that Australian banks are very big borrowers in overseas bond markets. This is because they source only about two-thirds of all the money they lend to Australians from bank deposits, which forces them to borrow the shortfall overseas. Consequently, Australian banks are vulnerable to what happens to overseas bond markets and global interest rates.

Bond credit quality

When managed funds and other investors consider investing in a bond, that is, they are considering if they should lend money to a government or a company, it is important that they assess the quality of the bond. This is done by reviewing what are known as bond credit ratings. Bond credit ratings attempt to give investors an indication of the likelihood of a bond issuer honouring their debts – that is, they are trying to predict the likelihood that the bond may go into default.

There are dozens of bond credit rating agencies around the world, but the major ones are Standard & Poor's, Fitch Ratings, Moody's, China Lianhe Credit Rating, China Chengxin, Capital Intelligence Ratings, Veda (now part of Equifax), Japan Credit Rating and Dun & Bradstreet. Different agencies have specialities in global bonds, government bonds, corporate bonds, bonds issued in growth economies, such as Russia, China and India, or bonds issued for special projects, such as alternative energy.

In Australia we think of government debt as being the highest quality given that Australia has the highest possible AAA credit rating. But this isn't true across the world as credit quality varies greatly all the way across the bond market and within segments.

Within governments, too, there are variations. Treasury debt, that is, bonds issued by governments, is usually considered the highest quality, with other government agencies (right down to local government) offering bonds of varying quality. Government debt can be issued both in the currency of the country (called local currency debt) or in some other currency (usually US dollars but also euros and yen).

Other companies at the bottom of the quality spectrum issue bonds that investors call "junk". Investors will still lend money to low-quality companies if the interest rates they receive are high enough to justify the high default risk.

Bond rating grades

Investment grade	Quality score
Aaa, AAA	Highest quality
Aa1, Aa2, Aa3, AA+, AA, AA-	High quality but some long-term default risk
A1, A2, A3, A+, A, A-	Medium quality but some negative concerns
Baa1, Baa2, Baa3, BBB+, BBB, BBB-	Medium quality but long-term warning signs
Non-investment grade	**Quality score**
Ba1, Ba2, Ba3, BB+, BB, BB-	Speculative fundamentals
B1, B2, B3, B+, B, B-	Invest with caution
Caa1, Caa2, Caa3, CCC+, CCC, CCC-	Poor quality, high default risk
Ca, CC	Low quality
C	Very low quality
D	In default

Source: Rainmaker Information

Maturity

Bond maturity refers to how long until the bond, or the debt, is fully repaid. For example, if you think of your house mortgage as a bond you have issued to the bank, its maturity is most likely 30 years. Maturities can be as short as one day or as long as 30 years (such as the 30-year Treasuries offered by the US government), although the Argentinian government has issued 100-year bonds. The popularity of these ultra-long-term bonds is even generating interest in the US, which is considering whether it should also issue 50-year and 100-year bonds.

Some bonds are offered in perpetuity, meaning they never have to be repaid but the issuer promises to keep paying the coupon forever.

One way to assess the bonds market is to examine what is known as the yield curve, which is a chart of how average interest rates vary according to their maturity. The yield curve is very useful because it gives investors an indication of market sentiment towards future interest rate movements. For example, the yield curve for Australian interest rates shows that while over the short term investors are happy to invest in bonds paying about 0.1%pa, to invest over the longer term they want higher rates of almost 1.0% to justify longer-term risks, such as their expectations that interest rates will eventually go up and long-term inflation. For comparison, investors in 100-year Argentinian bonds have been promised 8% yields.

How your managed fund makes money investing in bonds

When a bond issuer issues a bond for, say, $10 million with a five-year maturity paying a 3% interest rate yield, the bond by definition is worth $10 million because that is what the investor (the managed fund) paid for it, that is, loaned the issuer. But let's say the managed fund's investment manager believes inflation is about to increase from 2% to 3%, meaning the 3% yield is no longer 1% above inflation but just matching it. The investment manager will probably want to sell the bond and buy one paying a higher interest rate, perhaps 4%.

To achieve this the investment manager has to sell the bond, possibly for a loss. But the investor they sell the bond to will still receive the yield of 3% on the face value of the bond, being an interest coupon payment of $300,000 pa on the $10 million bond certificate. But if the new owner of the bond buys the bond for, say, $7.5 million, then the $300,000 interest yield payment would convert to an effective yield of 4%. So the first investor has suffered a 25% investment loss to get the poorly performing bond out if its portfolio only to see the new owner of the bond receiving an effective 4% yield.

This example illustrates how the prices of bonds, generally speaking, move in the opposite direction of yields (the effective interest rate). Put another way, when interest rates go up, bond prices fall, and when interest rates go down, bond prices go up.

If your managed fund is good at analysing and forecasting which way interest rates will shift, it is easy to see how it can make money for the fund – and for an investor in that fund.

There are also some basic mechanics around bond investments of which investors into managed funds that have a high emphasis on bonds should be aware. For example, when a bond is issued it has a fixed coupon that is paid every six or 12 months. The coupon amount is based on interest rates at the time of issue. The price of the bond is based on all the future cashflows coming from that bond, including the return of capital when the bond matures. If interest rates subsequently rise, future bonds will reflect those changes in the coupon paid.

As a result, the price of any existing bonds must fall so that the total return (coupons plus the return of capital or face value) to maturity is the same. The opposite happens when interest rates fall. The price of existing bonds rise so that anyone buying that bond will get the same return as someone buying a new bond with the same maturity.

However, long-maturity bond prices are more sensitive to interest rate changes than short-duration bonds because they have more cashflows in the form of future interest rate coupon payments compared with short-duration bonds. The price has to change more to compensate for this fact. This is known as interest rate risk.

Australian government bond yield curve – December 2021

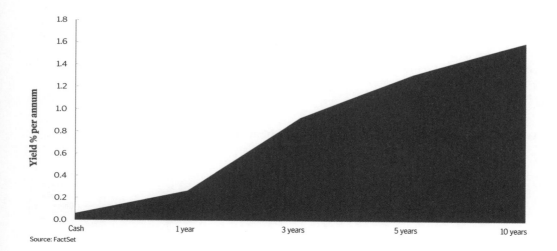

Source: FactSet

Capital return + interest payment = your bond's investment return

When you invest in a managed fund bond portfolio you make money in two ways: from the interest rate payments and the capital return, that is, the increasing capital value of the bonds in the portfolio. This makes bond investments more sophisticated than bank term deposits, which only pay you an interest rate.

Cash

Cash is an asset class that everyone thinks they understand until they have to start investing in it.

Cash is the currency notes and coins we carry around in our wallets and purses – or it used to be. Cash now includes not just physical money but electronic money in debit cards and other forms of e-payments. While we cannot earn a return on the cash we have in our hands, we can when the money is in the bank, a fund or in some type of short-maturity bond, for example, one that invests in the money market.

We've all heard the term "cash is king". That's because it is extremely liquid, meaning it can quickly and easily be converted into other assets with almost no probability of capital loss. In fact, sometimes we get discounts by offering to pay for items with cash because the seller gets paid straightaway and there's no possibility of default or a change of mind, and no other charges are involved.

Another feature is that while we've learned in other articles in this edition of *The Good Investment Guide* that investment returns come from both yield and capital

return, with cash there is no capital return – all the return is from its yield or interest rate. But with no capital growth the purchasing power of the initial investment reduces over time due to the effects of inflation.

In order to achieve returns higher than inflation, the after-tax cash rate must be above the inflation rate. This is why cash is considered low risk from a short-term capital preservation perspective, but higher risk over the long term because of the deterioration of the capital value from an after-inflation perspective, particularly if invested in a high tax environment (the tax rate does not take into account the effects of inflation).

The cash yield is based on the short-term interest rate set by a country's central bank – in Australia, this is the overnight money market interest rate set by the Reserve Bank of Australia (RBA). Over time the yield on cash varies in line with RBA monetary policy, with the key characteristics being absolute capital security, high liquidity and variable yield.

Official cash rates from across the world – December 2021

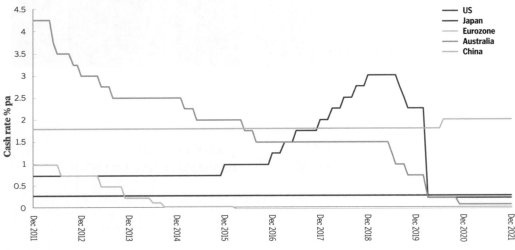

Source: FactSet

How to invest in cash

There are several ways to invest in cash. The first is straight out cash in the form of notes and coins. There is a cost involved in holding cash – it can be lost or stolen and provides no possibility of yield.

Bank term deposits

Investors can place their money in short-term bank deposits (called term deposits) for periods of up to three years. When they do this they give up liquidity and may suffer a break fee if they decide they need their money earlier than the term stated.

Credit funds

Investors willing to take slightly more risk may wish to deposit their money into a credit fund, which is like a term deposit but the fund is run by a non-bank mortgage lender. Some credit fund operators are highly regarded and quite safe but some are not, so you have to do your research.

Debentures

Debentures are unsecured credit funds offered by private companies. With debentures there is a much higher risk that the operator may not be able to honour your interest rate payments, let alone return your capital. Because these are unsecured, if the company you loaned your money to folds, there is no guarantee you will be repaid.

Mortgage funds

Mortgage credit funds offer yields above that of cash term deposits and most offer daily liquidity. But many of them ran into trouble during the global financial crisis because companies operating the mortgage funds had to sell the funds' underlying properties when their lenders called in their loans. This resulted in affected mortgage funds being frozen and investors unable to access their account.

Cash investment funds

Cash investment funds, which may include cash management trusts, are investment funds operated by some of Australia's biggest investment managers. These funds invest in very high-quality assets like bank bills, negotiable certificates of deposit (NCDs) and term deposits. Some are available as exchange traded funds. The largest of these is more than $1 billion in size.

KEY POINTS

- Cash is physical and electronic money that you can use for transactions.

- When you invest in cash you may only receive an interest payment because it does not earn a capital return.

- Bank term deposits, credit funds, debentures, mortgage funds, bank bills and negotiable certificates of deposit are all types of cash-based investments.

Bank bills and NCDs

Bank bills are special securities issued by banks and which are negotiable orders (that is, they can be traded) to pay a certain amount of money at a certain time in the future. They usually mature within six months. Bank bills are 100% guaranteed by the bank issuing the bills. In practical terms, bank bills are discount securities, which means they are issued at a discount to their face value but redeemed at their face value at maturity – in this way, the interest rate is built into the face value price.

NCDs are negotiable certificates of deposit. They are similar to bank term deposits but instead of the deposit being recorded in a bank account they are backed by a certificate that can be traded.

Alternatives

Alternative assets are those that don't easily fit into the mainstream asset class categories like equities, bonds, property or cash. While some alternative assets are exotic and higher risk, not all are. You need to understand each alternative investment case by case.

KEY POINTS

- Alternative assets are those that can't be easily classified into the mainstream asset class categories.

- The main types of alternative assets are hedge funds, infrastructure, private equity, venture capital and precious metals.

- Alternative asset investment strategies have lower liquidity than regular strategies, are associated with higher fees and require investment managers to be highly skilled.

When managed funds talk about their investments they usually focus on the mainstream asset classes such as Australian or overseas equities, government or corporate bonds, direct or listed property and cash. But for investments that are not so easy to classify we use the broad term of alternatives – they are an alternative to what is mainstream.

This doesn't make alternative assets high risk or speculative, although some can be. It just makes them harder to classify because by their nature they are different. After all, if they weren't we wouldn't need to call them an alternative asset.

Another way to look at alternative assets is that they behave differently from the traditional asset classes and from each other. For the individual investor, accessing them can be more difficult as well. Alternative assets can behave differently for two reasons.

First is that the physical underlying assets are different if they are, for example, infrastructure assets like bridges, airports, public utilities companies, emerging market high-risk credit bonds, or equity in privately held companies.

The second reason is that some alternative investment strategies don't focus on the underlying physical asset like mainstream investment strategies do, but rather on the investment process.

By this we mean that some alternative asset strategies emphasise complex trading strategies in highly liquid financial securities, such as futures and options across a variety of markets not limited to equities, currencies, fixed income and commodities. As a result they can profit from relative values between different securities, not just from whether the asset goes up or down in price.

For these reasons it is best that investors access alternative assets through pooled investments. Alternative assets tend to have low liquidity, meaning they cannot be quickly redeemed for cash, can have high fees and are generally associated with higher levels of investment risk. But on the upside, skilled alternatives investment managers can achieve high profits for investors.

Hedge funds

Hedge funds are specialist funds where the portfolio manager seeks to earn absolute returns rather than being bound by reference to an investable benchmark index. The underlying assets held in these funds and the trading strategies their investment managers use are often complex and may include trading financial instruments, investing in combinations of currencies, fixed income, commodities and precious metals.

Some hedge funds can be considered high risk because of their exotic trading strategies but some are low or moderate risk. Each hedge fund needs to be assessed on its merits because they are highly dependent on the skills and practices of the people running the fund.

Infrastructure

Infrastructure includes investments in assets such as airports, toll roads, electricity or water utilities, and bridges. They are usually associated with a sort of monopoly power, which cannot easily be replicated. For example, each city usually has one major airport or only a small number of electricity providers. Reflecting this, they are usually subject to government regulation that guarantees their revenue and legislates price increases. Due to their illiquidity, durable nature and protected revenue, they are generally held for many years. Infrastructure is considered moderately risky.

Private equity

Private equity is similar to investing in regular company shares except that the companies involved are privately held rather than being listed on the securities exchange. Private equity companies can include reasonably new companies still being prepared to be listed on a shares exchange or they can be previously listed public companies that were purchased by a private equity fund when the company was close to failing, the idea being to restructure the company and re-list it later for a large profit.

When a company is bought by private equity investors the new owners usually install their own management to restore the company and then sell it to new investors through either a trade sale or by listing it on the sharemarket. An investor may not know their overall investment return from a private equity investment until the company or portfolio of companies has been sold or listed on the sharemarket. As a result the private equity asset class is considered very high risk, requiring considerable expertise from the investment manager making these investments.

Venture capital

Venture capital is similar to private equity except it involves the financing of very young start-up companies that investors believe have high growth potential but no track record. The companies are usually from high-technology industries, such as information technology, clean technology such as in the renewable energy sector, or biotechnology. Venture capital funds provide funding and managerial expertise. On an individual basis they have a low rate of success, but this is potentially made up for by the companies that become spectacularly successful. Venture capital is considered high risk.

Precious metals

Precious metals such as gold, silver, platinum and palladium can be purchased for their intrinsic value and low correlation with traditional asset classes. They can be held physically in the form of ingots or through exchange traded funds.

Securities lending and short selling

A commonly cited example of alternative investing used by hedge funds is short selling. This is when a hedge fund manager believes a company's shares are about to sharply fall in value and sells them, even if they don't own any of the shares. To make the trade, the hedge fund manager has to borrow or rent the shares from another investment manager, superannuation fund or custodian so they can deliver the shares to the buyer at the agreed price. The hedge fund manager makes a profit if the price they sold the shares for is higher than the price of the shares when the time comes to return the borrowed securities. When a hedge fund manager engages in short selling they are betting a company's share price will plummet more than the buyer of the shares believes.

Short selling is extremely high risk and is heavily criticised because it encourages speculation in collapsing companies. However, if carefully executed, short selling trades can be highly profitable.

Investment styles

Investment style is the philosophy behind the investment strategy used by your managed fund's investment manager.

KEY POINTS

- Investment style is the philosophy behind your investment manager's strategy.

- There are four main styles – value, growth, neutral and indexed.

- Some styles have sub-variants and other styles are known by several terms.

These investment styles can be separated into active styles where the manager tries to outperform the market, or indexed styles where the manager tries to match the market. While investment managers like describing their investment styles in a multitude of ways, in reality most investment styles can be grouped into four main types, where the first three are active and the fourth is indexed.

Value

Investment managers that use the value investment style try to pick particular investments based on their analysis and judgement rather than the broader momentum of the market. These managers are sometimes referred to as stock pickers because they use their insight and expertise to pick particular stocks that they believe are likely to outperform regardless of the broader economic conditions. This style is sometimes described using the term "bottom-up".

Value or bottom-up investment managers base their judgements on analysis of how stocks rank according to traditional valuation methods, such as price to earnings (p/e), price to book value, price to net tangible asset backing (break-up value) and dividend yield. While value managers will still assess the growth potential and barriers to entry that a company may benefit from, the valuation factors dominate the investment screening and ranking process.

Value investors look for shares that are cheap relative to what the investor considers fair value. This might occur, for example, when an overall industry is struggling or in decline. While the prices of all companies in that industry fall, there might be some standout companies that investors have overlooked in their rush to exit all companies involved in that industry. Value investors step in when prices have fallen and take a long-term view that the company or industry will recover.

Growth

The growth investment style is sometimes referred to as momentum or thematic because investment managers that follow it seek to invest in stocks and securities that exhibit strong growth tendencies either in themselves or because the market is going through a growth phase.

These managers will analyse growth in profits, earnings and sales by focusing on industry factors, as well as barriers to entry for new entrants, the pricing power of the company and other factors that allow a company to sustain increasing profit margins. Broadly speaking, growth factors will dominate the investment screening and ranking process.

Growth investing is about investing in firms that are growing quickly. The companies may have low dividend yields because they reinvest nearly all their earnings in order to fund future growth. Growth companies are perceived as innovators. The companies may appear expensive based on their current earnings, but the investor predicts that future growth will make today's price look cheap in retrospect. The risk with these companies is that their growth rate may slow and the current high prices are not justified. Another risk is that expectations of future growth are built on false (or changing) assumptions or that the company mismanages its growth.

There are two variants of growth investing: momentum and market capitalisation.

The momentum investment style refers to the buying and selling of securities within shorter time periods, often by taking advantage of short-term price movements. Investment managers following a momentum style seldom do long-term in-depth analysis, relying instead on computer algorithms to make decisions for them based on price patterns, "moving averages" and differences in price based on similar securities. These investors often use what is called technical analysis, which involves charts using price and volume to pick turning points.

The market capitalisation investment style refers to the belief that certain segments of the stockmarket provide higher risk-adjusted returns than others. This may be because that segment suits their investment style. For example, many small cap investment managers believe that the segment is under-researched, which means there are potential bargains for active managers. Others believe large cap stocks provide higher returns because larger companies can be run more efficiently and there are barriers to entry in their particular industries.

Neutral

The neutral investment style is neither value nor growth. It seeks to avoid the strong biases that can be exhibited by these managers, aiming instead to add value regardless of which style of investment is in favour. These managers can have both valuation and growth factors within their screening and ranking. Despite a manager having a neutral style tendency, the investment process often leads to a portfolio with a slight bias towards value or growth.

Indexed

Indexed managers are those that don't try to outperform the market, but seek only to match it. They adopt this style because they believe that over the long term it is inherently difficult to outperform the market, a view supported by the finding that asset allocation is a more important influencer of long-term returns for diversified portfolios.

Indexed management also has the advantage of being much cheaper to implement because managers do not need to research the market to the same extent, preferring instead to put their energies into executing their trades as efficiently as possible.

While most indexed investment managers follow traditional measures such as the stockmarket index or a bond market index, they can also follow composite hybrid measures, such as an index based on, say, the most profitable companies, companies with the highest sales, companies that are most reliant on overseas revenue, and so on. Indexed managers should not be confused with passive investment strategies or styles, where an investment is placed and just left for the long term. Indexed management is about matching the market index as cost effectively as possible.

Value versus growth – two examples

The following charts demonstrate the difference between value and growth investing. The growth manager is looking for companies that will grow in earnings, with the price reflecting that growth. CSL Limited, which was privatised in 1994, is a great example of a growth stock. In the past 20 years earnings per share has grown from 14 cents per share in December 2000 to $6.91 in December 2020 – a growth rate of 22%pa. In that time the share price rose from $13 to $283 – a growth rate of 17% a year (this does not include dividend payouts).

Telstra Corporation Limited, on the other hand, is a good example of a value stock. It began the period with a share price of $6.43 and 20 years later was worth $2.98 a share – a negative return of 4% a year. Earnings per share fell from 29 cents per share to 15 cents per share.

CSL is a good example of a growth stock

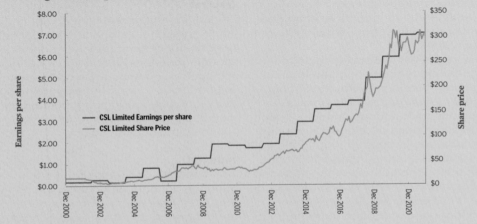

Telstra is a good example of a value stock

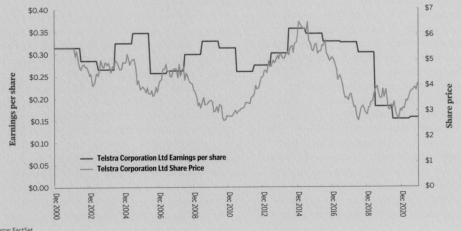

Source: FactSet

Indexed investing

Indexed investment management is when the managed fund's investment managers don't try to beat the market but aim to match it.

Indexed managers seek to match the market, rather than outperform it. This is based on the belief that, over the long term, it is difficult to outperform the market. Indexed managers take the view that asset allocation is the primary influencer of long-term returns for diversified portfolios.

A key advantage of indexed investment managed funds is that they have low costs because managers do not need to research the market to the same extent as active investment managers (the term we use to describe investment managers who do try to beat the market), preferring instead to focus on executing their trades as efficiently as possible. As a result, managed funds using indexed investment management strategies can have very low fees.

Most indexed investment managers follow traditional benchmark indices, such as a bond market index or stockmarket index. These measures are special price-based averages across the stockmarket where larger companies are given a bigger weighting in the index based on the total value of their company (that is, their market capitalisation).

Indexes followed by managed funds

The main way investors compare indexed managed funds is by understanding the market index they follow and their fees, and by examining their tracking error, which is a measure of how closely they replicate that index. As a result, when investors choose an indexed managed fund their most important decision is what index they wish to follow, noting that indexes with similar names can have different calculation methods or can focus on different parts of market.

The most commonly followed index benchmarks associated with managed funds that follow those indexes are described in the table on page 54. New indexes are, however, being developed all the time, for example, special indexes that attempt to follow the infrastructure market or even hedge funds.

KEY POINTS

- Indexed investment managed funds have low costs because they don't try to beat the market but match it.

- The most important decision when choosing an indexed fund is which index you want to follow.

- Many exchange traded funds follow indexed investment strategies.

Smart beta funds

Smart beta funds are special types of indexed funds that follow more complex composite or hybrid measures, such as an index based on, say, the most profitable companies, companies with the highest sales, companies that are most reliant on overseas revenue, and so on. The term smart beta is based on the word "beta", which analysts use to describe the average return across the market. Smart beta strategies are supposedly cleverer ways for investors to outperform the traditional market.

Proportion of investment market that follows indexing

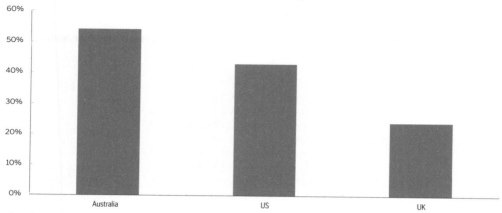

Source: Rainmaker Information

Common indexes used by Australian managed funds

Asset class	Index
Australian equities	S&P/ASX 200
	S&P/ASX 300
	MSCI Australian Shares Large Cap
International equities	MSCI World Index
	S&P 500
	Dow Jones Global Titans
	FTSE All-World index series
Property	S&P/ASX 200 A-REIT Index
Fixed income	Bloomberg Barclays Global Aggregate
	Bloomberg AusBond Composite Index
	Merrill Lynch US High Yield Master II Index
Cash	RBA Cash Rate Total Return Index
	Bloomberg AusBond Bank Bill Index

Indexed management ≠ Passive management

Indexed investment management is not the same as passive investment management. When an investment manager invests passively they buy a block of company shares, bonds or a property and just leave it in their portfolio. When an indexed investment manager buys shares, bonds or property it is because they wish to match or replicate the market or a particular segment of the market. This leads to the counterintuitive situation where index investment managers are actively deciding which indexes they wish to follow or be exposed to.

Exchange traded funds

An exchange traded fund (ETF) is a type of investment fund that combines some of the benefits of shares and managed funds. ETFs allow investors to access a portfolio of securities and are traded on the stock exchange. ETF portfolios are designed to replicate particular indexes, such as the ASX 200 or the S&P 500 in the US market. ETF portfolios may include Australian shares, international shares, fixed income securities, listed property trusts, or a combination of asset classes.

The price of the ETF reflects the price of the underlying assets, not the demand for the units in the ETF – that is, ETFs are exchangeable on securities exchanges but they are not listed like normal company shares are.

The structure of ETFs means they can often operate at lower management expense ratios (MERs) than regular managed funds. For example, while many managed funds may incur average fees of 1.5%, ETFs can operate with average fees of about 0.5%, and some can have fees as low as 0.1%. There are no entry or exit costs other than the broking charges.

There are two main types of ETFs:

1. Classical ETFs – based on and aim to match the performance of any one of a number of indexes. Classical ETFs use special off-market issue and redemption procedures to increase their attractiveness to institutional investors.

2. Hybrid ETFs – can either be based on an index or can be actively managed by the fund manager selecting the securities that they favour. Hybrid ETFs provide access to a much broader range of asset classes and investment management styles and strategies.

The key features and benefits of ETFs are:

- Investors can use them to directly access Australian or international sharemarkets at comparatively low cost. They can also access actively managed funds or funds that cover a specific sector of the market.
- ETFs use an open-ended structure and are designed to trade at or very close to their net asset value. This means the sharemarket price of an ETF should fully reflect the performance of the underlying portfolio, with no other factors affecting it.
- Regular income distributions are made to investors based on the amount of income generated by dividends, coupons and realised capital gains.
- ETFs pass their earnings onto investors untaxed, with the investor paying tax in the normal fashion. However, some of these earnings can be tax advantaged through franking credits earned by the underlying portfolio, and index-based ETFs do not generate significant realised capital gains due to their low portfolio turnover. If the ETF is held for more than a year, the investor is also eligible for the concessional rate of capital gains tax.
- Ease of access: ETFs can be bought and sold during ASX trading days and prices are continually updated throughout the day. Classical ETFs use special intra-day pricing mechanisms.
- The same buy/sell strategies used for shares can also be applied to ETFs, including placing orders at limit and using margin loans or instalment warrants to fund the investment.

ESG investing

Environmental, social and governance (ESG) or ethical investing is an investment methodology that seeks to invest in companies, properties or bonds that are aligned with the personal values of the investor.

KEY POINTS

- The framework for defining the ethical investment credentials of a managed fund are known as the United Nations Principles for Responsible Investment (UN PRI).

- Australia has the fourth highest number of investment companies that have signed up to these principles.

- Australian equities ethical investment strategies outperform over the short, medium and long term although the evidence for international equities is mixed.

The rise in awareness of climate change, concerns over pollution and alternative energy, deforestation, the harmful health effects of tobacco and excessive alcohol consumption, inequality and discrimination, and the scale of the global munitions industries have prompted some investors to direct their investments into managed funds that they believe will have a positive environmental and social impact.

When investors do this they are pursuing what are known as ESG or ethical investment principles. The subtlety with this style of investing is that what is ethical to one investor might not be ethical to another.

At its simplest, ESG investing avoids companies that do the most harm to both people and the environment. These include companies involved in gambling, alcohol, tobacco and guns. These are known as "sin" stocks. When investment managers avoid these companies in their portfolios, this is known as negative screening, that is, the focus is on determining which stocks should not be included.

An alternative approach is for investment managers to focus on or seek out companies that are the best in the market or at least their industry segment on environmental or social factors. This is known as positive screening.

Investors looking for managed funds that have an ESG investment philosophy have two broad choices:

1. Invest in a managed fund that is explicitly labelled ESG, that is, it selects constituent assets, such as company shares, bonds or properties using a combination of positive and negative screens.

ESG investment manager guidelines

When managed funds and their investment managers label themselves as ESG or ethical, and if they declare they follow UN PRI guidelines, they are agreeing to be bound by the following principles:
- They will incorporate environmental, social and governance (ESG) issues into their investment analysis and decision-making.
- They will be active owners of investment assets and incorporate ESG issues into their investment practices, including how they vote at company shareholder meetings.
- They will seek appropriate disclosure on ESG issues by the entities in which they invest.
- They will promote acceptance and implementation of the UN PRI within the investment industry and work together to enhance the effectiveness of the principles.
- They will each report on their activities and progress towards implementing the principles.

2. Invest into a managed fund where the investment manager may not use specific screens when choosing its assets because it instead uses an overarching ESG framework to guide how the managed fund operates. This is called using an ESG governance overlay.

These investment frameworks becoming more common prompted the United Nations in 2005 to establish the Principles for Responsible Investment (UN PRI) to formulate sets of environmental, social and governance guidelines around ethical investment and related overlays and to work with investment managers, superannuation funds, regulators, credit rating agencies and industry associations to promote these principles. This framework is known as ESG. Each ESG factor is described below:

Environmental concerns include screening out stocks that make their money from activities that are negative for climate change (such as coal-fired power plants). On the other hand, the ESG investment process looks favourably on businesses that profit from reducing the effects of climate change, such as alternative power strategies like solar or wind farms.

Social concerns include assessing a company's policies and commitment to diversity (such as its hiring policies), human rights (such as examining the company's supply chain to make sure people work in safe conditions and are paid a living wage) and animal welfare (in particular, testing products on animals).

Governance concerns include a special focus on how UN PRI signatories run their own businesses as well as how they select and seek to influence the companies in which they invest – for example, by participating in shareholder meetings and taking activist positions.

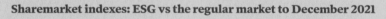

Do ESG investments outperform?

While investors may have personal preferences about ESG or ethical investment, managed funds and their philosophies, the key question is how do these investment strategies perform compared with regular investment strategies? As this chart shows, in Australia they underperformed over the short term but over the longer term they returned about the same. In international equities the result depended on the time period.

Sharemarket indexes: ESG vs the regular market to December 2021

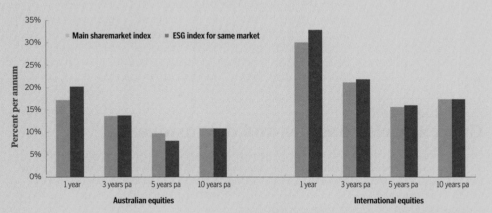

Indices in this chart: Australian equities, ASX/S&P 200 and the MSCI Australian ESG Leaders
International equities, MSCI All Countries in AUD and MSCI World ESG Leaders in AUD

Source: FactSet

How managed funds handle currency risk

Managed funds that invest overseas have currency risks because when they buy their foreign assets or receive income from that asset they have to do these transactions using foreign currencies. Misjudging these currency transfers can turn a seemingly profitable investment into a loss.

KEY POINTS

- When managed funds invest overseas they need foreign currency to make the transaction.

- Mismanaging currency risk can cost managed funds and their investors a lot of money.

- Managed funds can lock in their currency conversion rates using a process known as currency hedging.

Whenever a managed fund buys an overseas asset it has to pay for it using foreign currency, and when it brings income from that investment back to Australia it has to convert that income into Australian currency.

The chance that an investor suffers a loss due to adverse movements in the currencies of the foreign country versus the Australian dollar is known as currency risk.

This example illustrates how this can play out: say a managed fund buys $10 million in equities that are listed on the New York Stock Exchange (NYSE). To do this it has to convert its Australian dollars (AUD) into US dollars (USD). When it made the conversion 1 USD was worth AUD 1.33 – that is, 1 AUD was worth US 75 cents – so the AUD 10 million actually bought it a USD 7.5 million parcel of those equities.

Now say that the price of those foreign equities rose 20% over the next year from USD 7.5 million to USD 9 million. While this is a very good investment return, the real question for the managed fund is: how does this convert into AUD? To work this out we need to analyse the currency conversion change over the same timeframe.

In the 12-month period, if the AUD currency conversion rate against the USD went up from 75 cents to 85 cents, that is, each USD is now worth AUD 1.18 compared with 1.33 before, the USD 9 million equity placement would be worth AUD 10.62 million (USD 9 million x 1.18). This means that the 20% equity return on the NYSE after taking into account the 13% currency appreciation converts to an effective reduced return of 6.2%.

In this example the rising value of the AUD reduced the managed fund's investment return. But it works in reverse, too, because if the AUD had depreciated (that is, gone down) the investment return would have gone up because each USD

Currency risk upsides and downsides

Currency risks are not always bad news. When the AUD appreciates (goes up in value) it lowers the price of overseas assets (in AUD terms). But this rising AUD reduces the AUD value of any income these overseas assets generate. If the AUD depreciates (goes down in value) the price of new overseas assets goes up in AUD terms, but the AUD value of any income these assets generate goes up.

The more countries in which a fund invests, however, the more complex its currency risk.

would be worth more AUD than before. For example, if the AUD to USD conversion rate had gone down from 0.75 to 0.65, the 20% equity return on the NYSE would have converted to an effective return of 38% from an Australian dollar perspective.

This means that when managed funds invest overseas and buy overseas assets they are also making judgments (or bets) regarding what they think will happen to the value of the AUD on world currency markets. While most of the time currency exchange rates are fairly stable and reasonably predictable, there are periods when exchange rates change rapidly and dramatically. When this happens it can have large effects on the capital value of a managed fund's investments.

Reduce currency risk by hedging

Currency risk can be reduced or eliminated by something called currency hedging, which is when a managed fund buys insurance against the currency changing value. When an investor hedges a currency they agree to a futures or derivatives options contract that

locks in a particular currency conversion rate. While this sounds complex, in practical terms the investor is simply agreeing to buy back Australian dollars at a predetermined exchange rate. This way, if there is a change in the exchange rate it doesn't affect the investor.

Currency hedging costs money to set up and this cost reduces the net return of the investment.

Generally speaking, investments in international equities are purchased without currency hedging even though many international share managed funds have a currency hedged option. If the investor has a particular view on the valuation of the AUD they can choose between these options in order to reduce risk or increase their returns.

Investments in international fixed income are generally currency hedged. This is because the majority of fixed interest returns are expected to come from the coupon of the bond. Investors in fixed interest consider this a defensive asset and do not like capital values fluctuating due to movements in currency exchange rates.

Value of 1 AUD against major currencies – 2011-2021

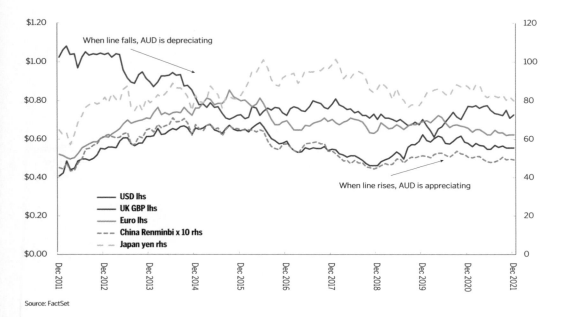

Source: FactSet

What is my investment risk profile?

Your investment risk profile is a description of what type of investor you are. This can encompass how much investment risk you are willing to take, your investment time horizon and what level of volatility (performance variability) you are prepared to accept.

Your investment risk profile depends on factors such as your goals, age, income and how much other money you have, and why you are investing, for example, are you saving towards a home deposit or a holiday in the next 12 months, to top up your superannuation or for your children's education?

When you know the answer to these questions you can begin mapping out an investment strategy because different asset classes possess different risk and return characteristics. These issues matter because you can justify why you would invest in, say, equities and real estate investment trusts which are higher risk than fixed income (bonds) investments and cash.

When trying to determine your risk profile it is useful to look at what the actual returns and level of risk have been from managed funds in the various investment asset classes over the years. The accompanying table and graph show that the higher the longer-term average investment returns, the higher the volatility.

This means that the higher the potential investment returns an investor seeks, the greater the risk or range of returns they must be prepared to tolerate. Your individual investment risk profile will therefore determine how much of your investment capital should be allocated to each asset class.

Generally speaking, investment experts will suggest

that you be allocated into one of five investment risk profiles based on your attitudes to risk and returns. It is important to note that the risk categories below are guidelines only, and some managed fund responsible entities or intermediaries, such as financial planners or brokers may adopt slightly different asset allocation ranges within the various risk profiles.

For example, some balanced investment funds may invest up to 85% of your money in equities and property. It is vital to read the fund's product disclosure statement to see what ranges within each asset class the fund may invest, depending on its mandate and targeted strategic asset allocation.

!

"Risk" to most people means the probability of losing some, or all, of your capital. But to investment experts risk means the likelihood of investment returns fluctuating excessively – which is why it's also called "volatility".

Managed fund asset class investment returns 20 years to December 2021

Asset class	Average return pa	Highest 12-month return	Lowest 12-month return	Range from highest to lowest
Australian equities	8.4%	44.7%	-40.0%	84.7%
International equities	6.8%	48.9%	-33.1%	81.9%
Australian REITs	7.2%	44.7%	-57.6%	102.3%
Australian fixed interest	5.4%	22.9%	-5.1%	27.9%
Cash	3.6%	7.5%	0.0%	7.5%

Source: Rainmaker Information

The five main risk groups:

1. Cash

One-hundrend per cent (100%) of your investment is invested in cash or cash equivalents. There is next to no chance of losing any of your capital, but the trade-off is that returns will be low although very predictable in the short term. The big risk is that your investment will not match inflation.

2. Conservative

Between 30% and 50% of your investment will be in the growth assets of equities and real estate investment trusts. There is a chance of a capital loss in any given year, but you can expect higher returns over the medium term compared with investing in cash. The investment will experience moderate levels of volatility.

3. Balanced

Between 55% and 75% of your investment will be invested in the growth assets of equities and real estate investment trusts. There is a greater chance of a capital loss in any given year, but you can expect higher returns over the long term compared with investing in the conservative risk profile. The investment will experience moderate to high levels of volatility.

4. Growth

Between 75% and 90% of your investment will be invested in the growth assets of equities and real estate investment trusts. There is an even greater chance of a capital loss in any given year, but you can expect higher returns over the long term compared with investing in the balanced risk profile. The investment can experience high to very high levels of volatility.

KEY POINTS

- Your investment risk profile depends on your goals, investment time horizon and how much risk you are prepared to tolerate.

- Different investment strategies, asset classes and managed funds are suitable for different types of investors.

- Understanding your own risk profile will help you decide which strategies, asset classes and funds are most suitable for you.

Managed fund asset class investment returns 20 years to December 2021

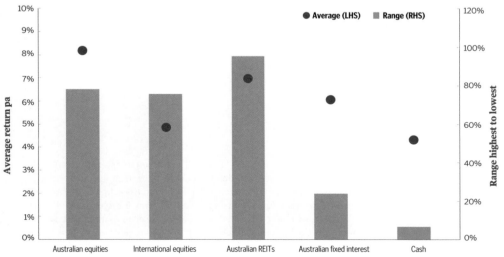

Source: FactSet

5. High growth

Typically 90% to 100% of your investment will be invested in growth assets, such as equities and real estate investment trusts. There is a high probability of a capital loss in any given year, but you can expect higher returns over the longer term compared with investing in any of the other risk profiles. The investment can experience very high levels of volatility.

To determine how you should allocate your money across these investments and asset classes according to your investment risk profile, you should ask yourself the following questions:

1. When will you require the money that you wish to invest? If you do not require access to the funds for at least five to seven years you can afford to have a greater exposure to equities and property in order to target a higher potential return. If you require the funds within five years, then it makes sense to have a lower exposure to equities and property, as you do not want to have to sell your investments after they have perhaps suffered a short-term drop in value due to adverse market conditions.

2. How would you feel emotionally if your investments suffered a sharp drop in value? If financial markets suffer extreme shocks, shares and listed property may drop by more than 20% in a given year. For example, there have been three occasions since 1970 in which Australian shares have finished the calendar year down by more than 20%. Within a given year, sharp falls can be even more common. If this is likely to cause you anxiety and worry, then you are not suited to having all of your money in shares. However, if you can accept a negative return once every five years, for example, then you may be more suited to a balanced risk profile. It is simply a matter of working out where you fit on the risk-return spectrum.

3. What other financial assets do you have? Do you have a large exposure to investment properties? Perhaps you should adopt a conservative approach, with your cash funds available for investment to balance things out. Are you 20 years away from retirement and looking for a suitable risk profile for your superannuation? Perhaps you can adopt a high weighting to growth assets. If you won't be requiring the funds for a long time, short-term falls in capital value are less of an immediate issue.

Buckets

Many investment professionals today advocate taking a "buckets" approach to determining a suitable investment risk profile. This means placing a certain amount of funds in the cash bucket for living expenses that may arise within the next two years, for such items as school fees, holidays, renovations and car repairs. If you have some funds that can be locked away for five to seven years, you should consider putting these funds into the balanced or growth bucket so that returns can be optimised over this longer timeframe. Cash funds that have an intermediate purpose may be best suited to the conservative bucket.

Should I see a financial adviser?

Financial advisers are professional experts who can help you understand your investment profile, design your investment strategy and choose managed funds.

Financial planning is a range of professional services that spans helping you understand your savings and investment goals and showing you how you can build and protect your wealth, how to set up the right financial structures and how to develop good financial habits that will position you for the future.

Financial planning can be delivered in person by a financial adviser, or it can be delivered in print, over the phone or online.

For investors, financial advisers can help provide independent advice on how you should invest yet protect your capital and build your wealth. This should also include advice on risk management, insurance and taxation.

Financial advice and managed funds

While information in this guide has been tailored to self-directed investors who are comfortable conducting their own research and making their own decisions and investment choices, not everyone is ready to do this by themselves.

This is why many investors, including highly experienced sophisticated investors, will have a relationship with a financial adviser, even if it is just to get a second opinion.

Choosing the right financial adviser

When choosing a financial adviser, make sure you find one who has all the necessary skills and qualifications, and who is part of a reputable advisory organisation committed to serving their clients' long-term needs. When considering which financial adviser to consult with, you should check:

- Are they a member of a relevant professional association? Members must abide by its code of ethics and rules of professional conduct.
- Are they registered with the ASIC Financial Advisers Register? Do they have an Australian financial services licence (AFSL)? Are they an authorised representative of an AFS licensee? If they aren't, then they aren't allowed to recommend investment products and you should not trust them.
- Their financial services guide (FSG) is like a product disclosure statement for financial advisers. Good ones will have it available on their website, and the FSG will contain all the information you need to understand who they represent, how they get paid, the services they provide and which companies they work with (this will help you spot potential conflicts of interest).

Financial services guide (FSG)

A financial services guide is like a product disclosure statement for financial advisers. It describes who an adviser represents, how they get paid, the services they provide and which companies they are associated with. Good advisers will have their FSG on full display on the website.

How do I choose the best managed fund?

Although not as important as determining your investment objectives or the long-run asset allocation for your portfolio, choosing the best managed fund can make a real difference both in terms of likely investment returns and the fees you will pay.

KEY POINTS

- There is a lot of available information on individual managed funds and you need to take the time to do some research.

- Intermediaries such as financial advisers and brokers have access to professional research and approved product lists.

- Headline investment returns are not everything, as sometimes they hide biases that can hurt your portfolio when the market changes.

- It is important to understand who will be looking after your investments, the credentials of their company and their investment track record.

Choosing managed funds can be one of the most complex endeavours an investor can undertake. But it doesn't have to be. The reason for the complexity is that there is a large and significant industry devoted to gathering your assets for management and charging you fees. While there is nothing wrong with that, it can make the task of selecting the best managed fund for your purposes more difficult. But with a bit of guidance and commonsense, most investors can navigate through this information to find good managed funds that will suit them.

While individual investors can do a lot of the research themselves, the most common approach is through the use of intermediaries, such as financial advisers or brokers, who have access to high-quality professional-grade research. This professional research comes from both within the organisation the intermediary belongs to and without (such as expert research houses). This ensures that recommended managed funds pass a minimum quality filter, which should protect the investor from products that would not be considered fit for purpose.

Individual private investors can still access a fair amount of quality information on individual funds using the internet. Managed fund product managers, responsible entities and investment managers have fact sheets and performance reports on individual funds that are updated regularly, usually on a monthly or quarterly basis. Note that if this information isn't easily available you should take it as a warning sign to be wary of investing in that managed fund.

While it is very important to assess managed funds' fees, the fees in themselves aren't so much the issue as what your investment return is after the fees have been deducted. You should be assessing investment performance against a relevant benchmark, for example, if the managed fund invests in Australian equities you should compare it against the Australian stockmarket index to gauge whether it is achieving returns above the index or if it is underperforming.

How the managed fund operates is also important, for example, is there an underlying investment manager of the fund and, if the managed fund invests, say, into international equities, does the Australian fund manager outsource this to global investment managers? This leads to the question of

Approved product lists

An approved product list is a formal menu or list of managed funds that your financial adviser or the advisory group they work for has researched and decided are high quality.

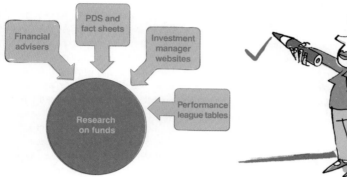

whether there is a coherent and clear explanation of how the fund has performed in the current market environment and why.

These major pieces of information should be contained in the managed fund's product disclosure statement (known as the PDS). This is the single most important document about the managed fund. While PDSs can vary in size and complexity, the product information they contain will be invaluable for helping you compare and contrast your managed funds.

What investment experts look for

A good guide when comparing managed funds is to think through what investment experts look for and to model your own comparisons on how they do their own research. Doing this might seem difficult, but by following the steps outlined below you will gain insights that will bring you very close to looking at managed funds just as the experts do.

- **Investment philosophy:** A manager's investment philosophy represents the firm's basic set of investment beliefs. For example, if it is an active investment manager their philosophy usually states that the manager believes markets are inefficient (meaning that the manager can outperform the markets after fees if it follows its investment process). Index managers, on the other hand, may not have an explicit investment philosophy other than saying their goal is to match the market index as closely as possible. Note, however, that some managed fund operators will have several funds and each may work differently, so understanding the breadth of these funds can also give you an appreciation of how they run their managed fund business.

- **People:** The quality of the investment executives and their staff, their relevant experience and formal educational qualifications are really important. While there are many qualified and experienced people in funds management, the more important goal is to weed out investment managers with dubious qualifications (or none at all). Another aspect of this is how investment teams are organised as some investment teams have lead portfolio managers who make all the decisions, while others have more collegiate teams where everyone is responsible for how portfolios are constructed. Look for investment managers with many years of experience and teams that have worked together for substantial periods of time.

- **Process:** This includes the approach that the investment manager uses to put its philosophy into practice. For example, if the manager strongly relies on going out to see individual companies and their management while building complex financial models, does the investment manager have the quality and quantity of resources (including people) needed to do this? If a more quantitative approach is taken using complex mathematical models, do they have the computing power, databases and intellectual rigour to put this into practice? If they are an index manager, do they have the systems in place to ensure trading costs are as low as possible?

- **Research:** This is about generating investment ideas, that is, an investment manager's ability to come up with insight and ideas about how other people's (your) money should be productively invested. In equities this is about reducing the number of companies in the investment universe to a manageable size. In high-yield fixed income this is about generating deal flow, meaning getting access to new issues of fixed-income securities. While managers should generate most of their ideas internally, it is worth knowing which external researchers they use and how this is paid for. Sometimes broker research is paid for by directing trades to that broker. If this is the case it is good for their fund manager clients to know.

- **Portfolio construction:** This involves (depending on the specific asset class) how the portfolio is constructed and within what limits. This could include weights to individual securities (whether shares or bonds), country weights, sector weights and limits to different credit ratings. The portfolio construction process should ensure the client gets the overall market return while giving the investment manager enough freedom to generate returns in excess of the benchmark index through their investment process and idea generation.

- **Ownership and funds under management:** Ownership by a large global group could be seen as an advantage due to stability and deep pockets which can provide development costs where needed. Alternatively, a small boutique manager, the number

of which has expanded significantly over the past 20 years, may be preferred due to the perceived greater skill and flexibility of the investment managers. Some investment insights only work on a small amount of money (relative to the size of the market). In some of the smaller, less liquid markets (such as small companies and distressed debt) managers can only manage so much money before their trading affects the market and their ability to generate excess returns – this is sometimes called the capacity constraint. Self-imposed limits on funds managed can give the investor confidence that the manager puts the investor before corporate revenue.

- **Performance:** While investment performance is, of course, an important factor, remember that you cannot buy past performance. Performance numbers show how the fund performed at a point in time during specific market conditions. If those conditions were repeated one would expect similar performance. However, market conditions are always changing. If a growth-oriented equities fund performed well when growth company shares were outperforming, you would not expect it to repeat that performance when value stocks are rising. It follows that if you believe future conditions would favour value stocks, it would be a mistake to go overweight in growth stocks.

Ranges of performance in Australian equities and international equities

The table on page 67 illustrates the range of returns available from active management in the two largest asset classes of the typical investor asset allocation – Australian equities and international equities. It compares the after-fees performance of actively managed funds over 1, 3 and 5 years (source: Rainmaker Information). In the case of Australian equities, the median fund underperformed over 1, 3 and 5 years, while the top quartile fund underperformed over 1 year, but outperformed over 3 and 5 years. This example helps to illustrate how difficult it is to beat a benchmark on a consistent basis. The standard deviation column shows that those funds that beat the benchmark index did so with higher volatility. The tracking error column – which measures the active risk bets the manager took in constructing the fund portfolio – also shows a correlation between how much risk the manager took on and the returns to the fund.

Some of the technical things that investment researchers might measure include:

- Relative performance (i.e., against an appropriate benchmark index).
- How much active risk was taken. This is measured by the difference between the fund return and the benchmark return (specifically, it is the volatility or the extent to which this gap changes).
- How much market risk was taken. This is measured by how much the investment return of the fund and the return of the benchmark tend to move in the same direction.

An investor in an actively managed fund wants both active risk (in order to generate outperformance) and market risk (to access the returns from the asset class).

- **Fees:** If you are paying fees above what you would pay for an index fund, you are paying for both the intellectual property of the manager (their unique investment insights) and the skill with which they implement their insights into your portfolio. Note that unique investment insights don't stay that way forever. If they work, they are often copied over time by other investment managers and can then be delivered at a lower cost. This is the free market at work, so don't overpay for something you can get more cheaply elsewhere. Some fees are difficult to

understand, particularly performance fees. If you don't understand the fee structure in a managed fund, be very cautious about whether that product is suited to your needs.

- **Back office and compliance:** This area does not necessarily directly affect performance but may relate to efficiency of trading and implementation of the investment decisions made. However, it does directly influence the quality, timeliness and accuracy of reporting to the investor.

Fund research factors to consider

Investment philosophy
People
Process
Research
Portfolio construction
Ownership
Funds under management
Performance
Fees
Back office and compliance

Active manager returns for periods to December 2021

	1 year	3 years pa	5 years pa	Standard deviation* pa (3 years)	Tracking error^ pa (3 years)
Australian equities					
Median	17.8	13.6	9.7	17.2	4.2
Index	17.2	13.6	9.8	17.1	
Outperformance	0.5	0.0	-0.1		
International equities					
Median	25.2	19.1	14.3	11.4	4.8
Index	29.9	21.0	15.5	11.4	
Outperformance	-4.7	-1.9	-1.2		

Source: FactSet, Rainmaker Information

Indexes: S&P ASX 200 - Index Total Return; MSCI AC World ex-Australia in AUD
*Standard deviation represents the volatility around the average return
^Tracking error is a measure of the risk taken by the manager versus the benchmark index

Monitoring your portfolio

After the hard work of establishing your investment goals, deciding your asset allocation and selecting your managed fund, comes the fun part: seeing how your individual investment decisions play out over time.

KEY POINTS

- Your investment portfolio should stay in line with your investment objectives.

- There are four aspects to monitoring your portfolio: performance, fees, asset allocation and goals.

- Staying on top of your portfolio enables you to change its structure as your needs change.

Monitoring your portfolio through time is an important part of investing. When done properly, it helps you make adjustments as needed and it helps you stay on track to meet your investment goals.

There are four aspects to monitoring your portfolio:

1. Performance

2. Fees

3. Asset allocation

4. Goals

The monitoring should be done using a spreadsheet or software you can access online through tools provided by your administration platform (if you have one). There are a number of free templates that will help you set this up, so you won't need to design these from scratch. Nevertheless, you should find the system that works best for you. Ideally the systems you use should have automatic links to your investments, but this will not always be the case. But as useful as having data in one place is, investors actually have to put it to good use to extract value from it.

Impact of fees on your portfolio's value

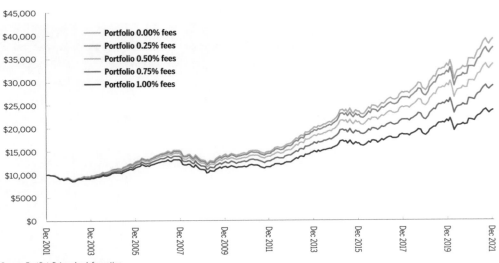

Source: FactSet, Rainmaker Information

Performance

The first and perhaps most obvious data point to track is a portfolio's performance. For this you need to track the performance of each individually held investment. These might be individual securities (shares, for example), or managed funds (unit trusts, ETFs, LICs).

Performance is generally provided to a recent point in time. For example, it might be over one month, six months, one year, three years or more. This is then compared with a relevant benchmark index. The index represents the asset class you are invested in (for example, Australian equities or fixed income). There are a lot of technical measures that can be generated by your software and these help give insight into the risks your portfolio is taking relative to the broader market.

One of the keys to performance monitoring is not to worry too much about a few underperforming investments. Remember that not all investments will outperform all the time. It might well be that the investments that are underperforming now will perform at different stages of the investment cycle, just as those that are currently outperforming will go through periods – sometimes for many years – when they will underperform.

The next step is to group together assets that are alike (by this we mean all investments in a specific asset class). The size of each investment is taken into account to produce a total overall asset class return. You will find that putting investments together from the same asset class will produce a return that is much closer to the asset class index than the returns from your individual securities or managed funds. This is diversification at work.

You should compare your total overall portfolio return against your investment objectives, returns target and whether you beat inflation by the amount you anticipated.

Fees

The second key item to track is the fees you are paying. All fees reduce the value of your portfolio, but expensive investment products, over time, can reduce a portfolio by tens if not hundreds of thousands of dollars.

The chart on the previous page shows the effect of different fee levels on a portfolio consisting of 30% Australian shares equities, 30% international equities and 40% bonds. The fund that pays 0.25% pa in fees has a final value of around $37,000. The portfolio with

---

Impact of fees on your portfolio's value when you make regular contributions

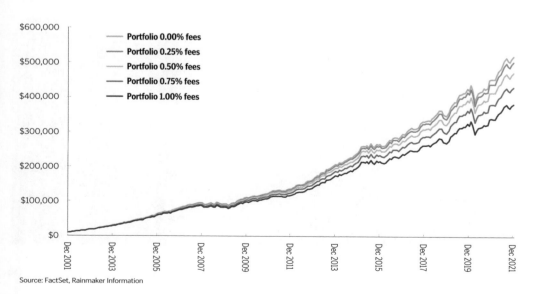

Source: FactSet, Rainmaker Information

fees of 1%pa (which is not unrealistic) has a final value of around $24,000 – around 35% less.

The chart below makes the example more realistic by introducing net positive cash flows of $10,000 a year. This makes it similar to a superannuation portfolio being built over 20 years that receives regular contributions. As a result you will note that the difference fees make in absolute terms is much greater. This is expected since the contributions to the portfolio make up a substantial part of the return (at $10,000 a year this equates to total contributions of $200,000 over 20 years). The portfolio with 0.25%pa fees ended up with a total value of $504,000 while the portfolio paying 1%pa fees had an ending value of $382,000. That's a difference of $120,000. For the average retiree that equates to around two years of living expenses.

Asset allocation

The third critical piece of information you need is the overall asset allocation of your portfolio. While you may have invested based on a perfect plan, your asset allocation will change as markets send some investments up and others down.

The chart below shows how asset allocation changes purely based on the relative returns of each asset class. Part of the job of monitoring your portfolio is ensuring that asset classes don't drift too far away from our intended asset allocation. After all, the asset allocation was designed to meet certain investment goals. That's a much harder job when they are out of balance.

Allowing asset classes to drift can cost you in terms of performance. The ideal is to use cashflows (whether adding to or redeeming assets) to maintain an asset allocation within your chosen limits.

Goals

Last but not least, it's important to evaluate a portfolio in light of our financial goals. While keeping an eye on performance, fees and asset allocation is important, it's pointless if we aren't on track to meet our goals for investing in the first place.

Some investment tracking tools also come with tools to track financial goals. For many, the goal will be retirement. For others, it might be to generate an income stream to fund a comfortable lifestyle (regular overseas travel, home renovation, purchasing a boat and so on). **M**

How investment returns can change your asset allocation

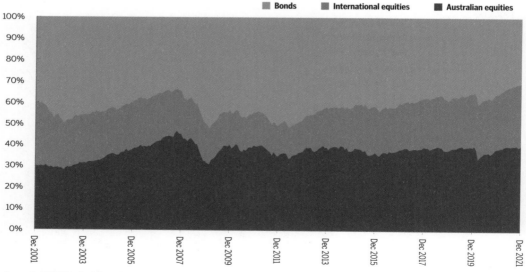

Source: FactSet, Rainmaker Information

MONEY MAGAZINE BEST OF THE BEST AWARDS 2022

Researching every managed fund in the market can be time-consuming and challenging. According to Rainmaker Information, there are more than 120 investment managers operating managed funds in Australia.

With this in mind, *Money* magazine's Best of the Best Awards recognise outstanding investment managers and products across major asset classes. Readers can use the following table of award winners as a reference point when selecting managed funds for their investment needs.

Money magazine's Best of the Best Awards 2022

It's no easy task to identify Australia's best (and best-value) managed funds. There were hundreds of product providers and thousands of products, choices and options to assess.

Rainmaker Information, publisher of *Money*, has been reviewing superannuation, managed funds and their investment managers for more than 20 years and this year Rainmaker Information again led the reviews and assessments for the Best of the Best managed funds awards.

When choosing a managed fund or exchange traded product (ETP), investors are not just looking for funds that scored the highest investment returns, but ones that also manage their investment risks. This includes an assessment of which managed funds most protect your capital.

This two-phase process requires Rainmaker to identify such factors as how much their performance changed month to month as well as how much and how often it went down versus up compared with the market and its peers. The next step is to study which funds get the highest returns per unit of risk.

This review was done over the short, medium and long term to June 30, 2021.

To be eligible for the awards, managed funds and ETPs must have minimum investments that are within the reach of most *Money* readers, or they must be accessible through a platform or the ASX. The best investment managers are those that have the most funds shortlisted in the most major categories.

Winners and finalists

BEST INVESTMENT MANAGER

WINNER 2022

Vanguard Investments Australia

It's fitting that Vanguard Investments Australia has taken out top spot as this year's best investment manager, having just notched up a quarter of a century serving investors in Australia.

With $35 billion in assets, the champion of low fees and simplicity is encouraging its investors to develop a long-term strategy when they build their portfolios.

The Vanguard brand is synonymous with exchange traded funds (ETFs). And for good reason: it is the largest ETF provider in Australia.

Vanguard recently made a strategic decision to step away from tailored institutional product offerings and instead increase its focus on improving outcomes for investors either directly or through the like-minded advisers that serve them.

Notably, Vanguard won the award for best fixed-interest ETF. It offers a range of seven fixed-interest ETFs for Australian investors, including corporate bonds, government bonds, as well as Australian, global and ESG offerings.

BEST LISTED REAL ASSETS FUND

Finalists

Vanguard Global Infrastructure Index Fund

Lazard Global Listed Infrastructure Fund

Alpha Infrastructure Fund

4D Global Infrastructure Fund

WINNER 2022

ClearBridge Investments RARE Infrastructure Fund – Hedged

BEST SMALL COMPANIES FUND

Finalists

Macquarie Australian Small Companies Fund

Perpetual Wholesale Smaller Companies Fund

OC Micro-Cap Fund

Alpha Aust Small Companies Fund

WINNER 2022

First Sentier Wholesale Australian Small Companies Fund

BEST AUSTRALIAN LISTED PROPERTY FUND

Finalists

Pendal Property Securities Fund
Ironbark Paladin Property Securities Fund
UBS Property Securities Fund
Alpha Property Securities Fund

WINNER 2022

Charter Hall Maxim Property Securities Fund

BEST AUSTRALIAN SHARE FUND

Finalists

Aberdeen Standard Focused Sustainable Australian
    Equities Fund
Ausbil 130/30 Focus Fund
Alphinity Sustainable Share Fund
Macquarie Australian Share Fund

WINNER 2022

Greencape Wholesale Broadcap Fund

BEST INTERNATIONAL SHARE FUND

Finalists

Intermede Global Equities Fund
Alphinity Global Equity Fund
LEGG Mason Martin Currie Global Long-Term
    Unconstrained Fund
BNP Paribas C WorldWide Global Equity Trust

WINNER 2022

Nikko AM Global Share Fund

BEST INCOME FUND

Finalists

Plato Australian Shares Income Fund
Lincoln Wholesale Australian Income Fund
Vanguard Australian Shares High Yield ETF
BetaShares Aust Top 20 Equity Yield Max Fund

WINNER 2022

First Sentier Wholesale Equity Income Fund

BEST AUSTRALIAN FIXED-INTEREST FUND

Finalists
Vanguard Aust Corporate Fixed Interest Index ETF
Pendal Enhanced Credit Fund
Franklin Aust Absolute Return Bond Fund (W Class)
Mason Stevens Credit Fund

WINNER 2022
Ardea Real Outcome Fund

BEST MULTI-SECTOR FUND

Finalists
IOOF MultiMix Balanced Growth Trust
Perpetual Diversified Real Return Fund - Class W
MLC Wholesale Inflation Plus-Assertive Portfolio
BlackRock Global Allocation Fund (Aust)

WINNER 2022
Macquarie Balanced Growth Fund

BEST CREDIT FUND – MORTGAGES

WINNER 2022
La Trobe 12-Month Term Account

MANAGED FUNDS PROVIDERS

So which managed funds are right for you?

There is more to consider than just a managed fund's performance. What is the minimum investment amount, what is the asset class and the portfolio holdings summary, where can you access these funds, what are the fees, how often will you be paid distribution payments and plenty more.

The following pages offer a key overview of some of *Money*'s Best of the Best managed fund winners for 2022, providing an even playing îeld to help you in your decision making.

FUND VALUE
AU$575.45m^

AT A GLANCE

APIR Code FID0031AU

Year established 2013

Product type Unit trust

Asset Class International equities

Minimum investment $25,000

Volatility/Risk level Very high

Distribution frequency Annually

Fund manager name
Amit Goel / Punam Sharma

Fidelity Global Emerging Markets Fund

fidelity.com.au

Overview

Investing in emerging markets can provide a unique opportunity to tap into some of the fastest-growing economies in the world. But what if the best opportunities are the ones that are harder to see? We prefer a more prudent approach, designed to provide more sustainable results over time.

The Fidelity Global Emerging Markets Fund gives investors access to a diversified portfolio of 30 to 50 quality companies in emerging markets. The Fund is actively managed, which means investors access a portfolio of carefully selected, globally listed securities exposed to emerging markets, which may or may not be in the Fund's benchmark.

The portfolio managers seek companies with a track record of robust corporate governance; selecting companies we believe are well positioned to generate returns through market cycles. With access to research and insights from 400 investment professionals worldwide, the Fund's investment experts have been finding some of the best opportunities in this exciting and dynamic region for more than 15 years.

Key features

- The Fund is a concentrated portfolio of our best 30 to 50 ideas in emerging markets.
- We are focused on providing investors with attractive returns over time.
- We use a rigorous bottom-up stock selection process using research from 400+ investment professionals around the world.
- We focus on finding companies well positioned to generate returns through market cycles with a track record of strong corporate governance.
- It is a concentrated portfolio with low turnover and a patient approach, which allows opportunities to come to fruition.
- Our portfolio construction process is based on our conviction of quality and returns over time.
- The Fund leverages unique local insights from 47 analysts in emerging markets.
- We've been investing in emerging markets for more than 15 years and have deep local knowledge.
- A team of portfolio managers that harnesses deep and collective knowledge of emerging markets.
- Available as an Unlisted Fund or ASX Quoted Fund: FEMX

Extra benefits available

Visit our website www.fidelity.com.au to:
- Register to receive our monthly insights newsletter from our global investment experts
- Learn more at our Learning hub on Active ETFs, sustainable investing and other investment concepts
- Register for free investor webinars.

^ As at 12 April 2022

Platforms

- Asgard
- BT Panorama
- Clearview
- First Wrap
- Hub24
- IOOF Pursuit
- Macquarie Wrap
- Mason Stevens
- Navigator MLC Wrap
- MyNorth
- Netwealth
- OneVue
- PortfolioCare
- Powerwrap
- Praemium
- WealthO2
- Xplore Wealth

Fees and holdings	
Entry/exit fee	Nil
Management fee	0.99%pa
Performance fee	Nil
Buy/Sell spread %	0.30% / 0.30%
Portfolio holdings#	Information technology: 30.6% Financials: 20.1% Consumer discretionary: 16.7% Industrials: 9.5% Consumer staples: 8.1% Materials: 8.0% Communication services: 2.4% Energy: 0.0% Healthcare: 0.0% Real estate: 0.0% Utilities: 0.0%

As at February 28, 2022. Portfolio information is included for illustration purposes only and may not represent actual holdings in the portfolio at the time of viewing. Due to rounding, some holdings in the Fund may appear as 0.0% of the Fund and the total holdings may not add up to 100%.

Performance*	1 year	3 years pa	5 years pa	7 years pa	Since inception
Net performance	-6.79%	10.02%	11.88%	8.77%	10.00%
Index: MSCI Emerging Market (Net Dividend) in AUD	-10.10%	3.01%	6.31%	4.95%	6.35%
Gross returns vs index	3.35%	7.01%	5.57%	3.82%	3.65%

* As at March 31, 2022.

CONTACT

Phone
1800 044 922

Email
auclientservices@fil.com

Mailing address
Level 17, 60 Martin Pl
Sydney NSW 2000

FUND VALUE
$ 5,428.7m

AT A GLANCE

APIR Code (12MTA) LTC0002AU

ARSN 088 178 321

Year established 2002

Product type Pooled

Asset Class Variable interest

Minimum investment $10.00

Volatility/Risk level Low-medium

Distribution frequency Monthly

Fund manager name
La Trobe Financial
Services Pty Limited

La Trobe Australian Credit Fund – 12 Month Term Account

latrobefinancial.com.au

Overview

The 12 Month Term Account is designed to take advantage of the outstanding risk/return characteristics of the Australian property credit market. The conservative investment strategy of the 12 Month Term Account is based on La Trobe Financial's seven decades of property credit experience. It aims to provide reasonably consistent, low volatility, variable monthly income for investors at all times throughout the cycle.

As Australia's most awarded property credit fund, the 12 Month Term Account provides investors with access to a diversified portfolio of high-quality credit assets and variable returns that are responsive to inflation.

Since inception in October 2002, the 12 Month Term Account has experienced no capital loss for investors. With a minimum investment of just $10 and no entry or exit fees if held to maturity, the 12 Month Term Account allows investors to gain exposure to this strong asset class to diversify their portfolio holdings with an award-winning, low-volatility, variable income solution.

Key features

- One of Australia's leading credit asset managers.
- No capital loss to investors since inception.
- All monthly distributions paid on time and in full since inception.
- All maturity redemptions made on time and in full since inception.
- Proven resilience and performance through market cycles and economic events.
- The 12 Month Term Account aims to provide regular variable monthly income to investors.
- High-quality asset selectively chosen and assessed by La Trobe Financial's experienced credit analysts.
- Transparent and consistent reporting available on website updated monthly.
- Online access available for all investors.

Fees and holdings

Entry/exit fee	No entry fees. Nil exit fees if held to maturity.
Management fee	1.60%
Performance fee	Nil
Buy/Sell spread %	N/A
Performance benchmark	Index: Bloomberg AusBond Bank Bill Index + 1.5%
Portfolio holdings summary %*	88.30% Domestic Fixed Interest 11.70% Cash From https://www.morningstar.com.au/Fund/FundReportPrint/14260

Performance*	1 year	3 years p.a.	5 years p.a.	7 years p.a.	10 years
Net performance	4.39%	4.79%	5.01%	5.13%	5.63%
Index: Bloomberg AusBond Bank Bill Index + 1.5%	1.53%	2.13%	2.61%	2.95%	3.48%
Gross returns vs. index	2.86%	2.66%	2.40%	2.18%	2.15%

* As at December 31, 2021. Past performance is not a reliable indicator of future performance.

La Trobe Financial Asset Management Limited ACN 007 332 363 Australian Financial Services Licence 222213 Australian Credit Licence 222213 is the responsible entity of the La Trobe Australian Credit Fund ARSN 088 178 321. It is important for you to consider the Product Disclosure Statement for the Credit Fund in deciding whether to invest, or to continue to invest, in the Credit Fund. You can read the PDS and the Target Market Determinations on our website or ask for a copy by calling us on 13 80 10.

For a full list of our awards, please visit the Awards and Ratings page on our website.

CONTACT

Phone
1800 818 818

Email
investor@latrobefinancial.com.au

Mailing address
GPO Box 2289
Melbourne VIC 3001

FUND VALUE
$10,770m^

AT A GLANCE

APIR Code MGE0001AU

ASX: MGOC

Year established 2007

Product type Unit Trust

Asset Class International equities

Minimum initial investment
$10,000 (when applying directly
with the Responsible Entity)

Volatility/Risk level Medium

Distribution frequency
Bi-annual

Fund manager name
Magellan Asset Management
Limited

Magellan Global Fund (Open Class) (Managed Fund) (ASX: MGOC)

magellangroup.com.au

Overview

Investing in 20-40 of the world's best companies, the fund aims to achieve attractive risk-adjusted returns over the medium to long term while reducing the risk of permanent capital loss.

Magellan's Global Equities strategy offers investors the opportunity to invest in a specialised and focused global equity portfolio. The Global Equities strategy's investment objective is to achieve attractive risk-adjusted returns over the medium to long term while reducing the risk of permanent capital loss. To achieve this, Magellan undertakes rigorous company research to identify what it assesses to be high-quality companies with enduring competitive advantages. This, combined with an assessment of the macroeconomic environment and a disciplined risk-controlled approach to portfolio construction, results in a focused portfolio of high-quality global equity stocks.

The Global Equities strategy is available in listed and unlisted form and where foreign currency exposures are hedged, unhedged or at the discretion of the manager.

Key features

- An actively managed fund investing in 20 to 40 of the world's best global stocks.
- Investment objective is to achieve attractive risk-adjusted returns over the medium to long term.
- The Fund aims to deliver 9%pa net of fees over the economic cycle.
- Aims to minimise the risk of a permanent capital loss.
- Target cash distribution of 4%pa, paid semi-annually.
- Invest via listed ASX: MGOC or unlisted MGE0001AU.
- Investors can buy or sell units on ASX (ASX: MGOC) or apply and redeem directly with the Responsible Entity (MGE0001AU).
- 'Open-ended' unit class of the Magellan Global Fund.
- Foreign currency exposure unhedged. Currency hedged version available.
- Minimum initial investment $10,000 when applying directly with the Responsible Entity.
- Minimum investment set by trading platform for listed version (typically $500).

Fees and holdings	
Entry/exit fee	No entry/exit fee, however transaction costs (that is, buy/sell spread) apply
Management fee	1.35%pa
Performance fee	10.0% of the excess return of the units of the Fund above the higher of the Index Relative Hurdle (MSCI World NTR Index (AUD)) and the Absolute Return Hurdle (the yield of 10-year Australian Government Bonds). Additionally, the performance fees are subject to a high water mark.
Buy/Sell spread %	0.07%/0.07%
Performance benchmark	MSCI World Net Total Return Index (AUD)

Portfolio holdings summary^	
Sector	
Information technology	24.0%
Consumer staples	20.5%
Consumer discretionary	14.1%
Cash	9.1%
Communication services	8.8%
Financials	8.1%
Healthcare	5.81%
Utilities	4.4%
Real Estate	3.8%
Industrials	1.4%

^ As at April 30, 2022

Platforms

Unlisted MGE0001AU

- Asgard eWrap
- Asgard
- AMP Flexible Solutions (FS) Range
- AMP Personalised Portfolio Service
- AMP Wealthview eWrap
- PortfolioCare (Hillross)
- North/MyNorth (AMP, Summit Synergy)
- ANZ OneAnswer
- ANZ Grow Wrap
- BT Wrap

- BT Panorama
- Colonial FirstChoice
- Colonial First Wrap
- HUB24
- IOOF Pursuit
- Macquarie Wrap
- Macquarie Accumulator
- MLC Wrap/Navigator
- uXchange
- MasonStevens
- PowerWrap
- Netwealth

Listed ASX: MGOC

- Asgard eWrap
- Asgard
- AMP Wealthview eWrap
- PortfolioCare (Hillross)
- North/MyNorth (AMP, Summit Synergy)
- BT Wrap
- BT Panorama

- Colonial First Wrap
- HUB24
- IOOF Pursuit
- Macquarie Wrap
- Macquarie Accumulator
- MLC Wrap/Navigator
- Mason Stevens
- Netwealth

CONTACT

Phone
1800 6243 5526

Email
clientservices
@magellangroup.com.au

Mailing address
Level 36, 25 Martin Place,
Sydney NSW 2000

MAGELLAN
EXPERTS IN GLOBAL INVESTING

FUND VALUE
$2,892m^

AT A GLANCE

APIR Code MGE0002AU

Year established 2007

Product type Unit Trust

Asset Class International equities

Minimum initial investment
$10,000

Volatility/Risk level Medium

Distribution frequency
Bi-annual

Fund manager name
Magellan Asset Management
Limited

Magellan Infrastructure Fund

magellangroup.com.au

Overview

The Magellan Infrastructure Fund has been designed to provide investors with efficient access to the infrastructure asset class, while reducing the risk of permanent capital loss. The infrastructure asset class, when appropriately defined, is characterised by monopoly-like assets that face reliable demand and enjoy predictable cashflows. As a result, Magellan has established proprietary classification criteria to appropriately categorise securities as investment grade infrastructure, and thus eligible for inclusion in its portfolios or otherwise. Potential investments that meet these criteria are expected to achieve strong underlying financial performance over medium- to long-term timeframes, which should translate into reliable, inflation-linked investment returns.

Magellan believes that an appropriately structured portfolio of 20 to 40 investments can provide sufficient diversification to ensure that investors are not overly correlated to any single company, industry-specific or macroeconomic risk. Magellan also offers the Magellan Infrastructure Fund (currency dedged) (the ASX quoted version of the Magellan Infrastructure Fund) and the unlisted Magellan Infrastructure Fund (unhedged).

Key features

- An actively managed fund investing in 20 to 40 of global listed infrastructure and utility stocks.
- Investment objective is to achieve attractive risk-adjusted returns over the medium to long term.
- Aims to reduce the risk of a permanent capital loss.
- Target cash distribution of 4%pa, paid semi-annually.

- 'Open-ended' unit class.
- Foreign currency exposure hedged. Currency unhedged version available.
- Minimum initial investment $10,000 for unlisted.
- Minimum investment set by trading platform for listed version (typically $500).

BEST LISTED REAL ASSETS FUND
Money
MAGAZINE
WINNER
2021
BEST OF THE BEST 2021

Fees and holdings	
Entry/exit fee	No entry/exit fee, however transaction costs (that is, buy/sell spread) apply
Management fee	1.05%pa
Performance fee	10.0% of the excess return of the units of the Fund above the higher of the Index Relative Hurdle (S&P Global Infrastructure Net Total Return Index (A$ hedged)) and the Absolute Return Hurdle (the yield of 10-year Australian Government Bonds). Additionally, the performance fees are subject to a high water mark.
Buy/Sell spread %	0.15% / 0.15%
Performance benchmark	S&P Global Infrastructure Net Total Return Index (A$ hedged)

Portfolio holdings summary^	
Sector	
Utilities	48.4%
Industrials	37.8%
Real Estate	8.7%
Energy	3.1%
Cash	2.0%

^ As at 30 April 2022

Platforms

- Asgard eWrap
- Asgard
- PortfolioCare (Hillross)
- North/MyNorth (AMP, Summit Synergy)
- ANZ Grow Wrap
- BT Wrap
- BT Panorama
- Colonial FirstChoice
- Colonial First Wrap
- HUB24
- IOOF Pursuit
- Macquarie Wrap
- Macquarie Accumulator
- MLC Wrap/Navigator
- uXchange
- Mason Stevens
- PowerWrap
- Netwealth

CONTACT

Phone
1800 6243 5526

Email
clientservices
@magellangroup.com.au

Mailing address
Level 36, 25 Martin Place,
Sydney NSW 2000

Now that you know more about managed funds...

Track the top performers with *Money's* comparison tables

View performance across asset classes over 1, 3, 5, 7 and 10 years

INVESTMENT MANAGER DIRECTORY

An A-Z listing of Australia's providers of unit trusts and exchange traded funds (ETFs).

Name	Telephone	Web address
abrdn Australia	1800 636 888	abrdn.com/en/australia/investor
Acadian Asset Management (Australia)	02 9093 1000	acadian-asset.com
Affluence Funds Management	1300 233 583	affluencefunds.com.au
Agora Asset Management	03 9652 9700	agoraam.com.au
AIMS Funds Management	02 9217 2727	aims.com.au
Airlie Funds Management	02 9235 4760	airliefundsmanagement.com.au
AIM	02 8379 3700	aimfunds.com.au
Alceon Real Estate	02 8023 4000	alceonre.com.au
Alexander Funds Management	1300 138 401	alexanderfunds.com.au
Allan Gray Australia	1300 604 604	allangray.com.au
AllianceBernstein	02 9255 1299	web.alliancebernstein.com/investments/au/portal.htm
Alpha Fund Managers	03 5406 5000	alphafundmanagers.com.au
Alphinity Investment Management	13 51 53	alphinity.com.au
Altius Asset Management	1300 590 488	altiusam.com
Altrinsic Global Advisors	02 8274 4835	altrinsic.com
AMP Capital Investors	1800 658 404	ampcapital.com.au
Antares	1300 738 355	antarescapital.com.au
Antipodes Partners	1300 010 311	antipodespartners.com
Aoris Investment Management	02 8098 1504	aoris.com.au
APN Funds Management	1800 996 456	apngroup.com.au
AQR	1800 778 019	australia.aqr.com
Aquasia	02 8061 4888	aquasia.com.au
Ardea Investment Management	13 51 53	ardea.com.au
Atlas Funds Management	02 8304 5190	atlasfunds.com.au
Atlas Infrastructure	02 8318 7639	atlasinfrastructure.com
Atrium Investment Management	02 9248 8090	atriuminvest.com.au
Ausbil Investment Management	1800 287 245	ausbil.com.au
Auscap Asset Management	02 8378 0800	auscapam.com
Australian Ethical Investment	1800 021 227	australianethical.com.au
Australian Unity	13 29 39	australianunity.com.au/wealth
Aviva Investors		avivainvestors.com/en-au
Barrow Hanley Global Investors	+1 214 665 1900	barrowhanley.com
Bell Asset Management	1300 305 476	bellasset.com.au
Bennelong	1800 895 388	bennelongfunds.com
Bentham Asset Management	13 51 53	benthamam.com
BlackRock	1300 366 100	blackrock.com/au
BMO Global Asset Management	02 9293 2804	bmogam.com/au-en/intermediary
BNP Paribas Asset Management Australia	1800 267 726	bnpparibas-am.com.au

Bombora	0438 648 980	bomboragroup.com.au
Brandes Investment Partners, L.P.	1 800 237 7119	brandes.com
Brandywine Global Investment Management	+1 21 609 3500	brandywineglobal.com
Capital Group	1800 026 192	capitalgroup.com/individual-investors/au/en
Centuria Capital	1300 505 050	centuria.com.au
Channel Capital	1800 940 899	channelcapital.com.au
Charter Hall Group	02 8651 9000	charterhall.com.au
Claremont Global		claremontglobal.com.au
ClearBridge Investments	02 9397 7300	clearbridgeinvestments.com.au
Clearwater Portfolio Management		clearwaterpm.com.au
Clime	1300 788 568	clime.com.au
Colchester Global Investors Inc.	+44 20 7292 6920	colchesterglobal.com
Cooper Investors	03 9660 2600	cooperinvestors.com
Copia Investment Partners	1800 442 129	copiapartners.com.au
Cromwell Funds Management	1800 334 533	cromwell.com.au
Daintree Capital	1300 011 088	daintreecapital.com.au
Dalton Street Capital	1300 074 894	daltonstreetcapital.com
Dexus	02 9017 1100	dexus.com
Dimensional Fund Advisors	02 8336 7100	au.dimensional.com
DNR Capital	07 3229 5531	dnrcapital.com.au
Dundas Global Investors	+44 131 556 2627	dundasglobal.com
DWS	1800 034 402	dws.com
ECP Asset Management	02 8651 6800	ecpam.com
EG Funds Management	02 9220 7000	eg.com.au
Eiger Capital	13 51 53	eigercapital.com
Eley Griffiths Group	02 8311 5175	eleygriffithsgroup.com
Ellerston Capital	02 9021 7797	ellerstoncapital.com
Elston Asset Management	1300 357 866	elston.com.au
Fairlight Asset Management	02 8231 6486	fairlightam.com.au
Fairview Equity Partners	03 9929 9441	fairviewequity.com.au
Fidelity International	1800 044 922	fidelity.com.au
Fiducian Portfolio Services	1800 653 263	fiducian.com.au
Firetrail Investments	1300 010 311	firetrail.com
First Sentier Investors	02 9010 5200	firstsentierinvestors.com.au
Flinders Investment Partners	03 9909 2690	flindersinvest.com.au
Forager Funds Management	02 8277 4812	foragerfunds.com
Franklin Templeton Investments Australia	03 9603 1200	franklintempleton.com.au
GMO Australia	02 8274 9900	gmo.com
GQG Partners		gqgpartners.com

Greencape Capital	13 51 53	greencapecapital.com.au
GSFM	02 9324 4356	gsfm.com.au
Hyperion Asset Management	1800 550 291	hyperion.com.au
Impax Asset Management Group plc	+44 20 7434 1122	impaxam.com
India Avenue Investment Management Australia	02 8245 0506	indiaavenueinvest.com
Insight Investment	02 9260 6645	insightinvestment.com/australia
Insignia	1800 062 963	ioof.com.au
Intermede Investment Partners	+44 20 3763 5810	intermede.co.uk
Invesco	1800 813 500	invesco.com.au/home
Investa Property Group	02 8226 9300	investa.com.au
Investors Mutual	1300 551 132	iml.com.au
Ironbark Asset Management	1800 034 402	ironbarkam.com
ISPT	03 8601 6666	ispt.net.au
Janus Henderson Investors (Australia)	1300 019 633	janushenderson.com/en-au/investor
JP Morgan Asset Management (Australia)	1800 576 468	am.jpmorgan.com/au/en/asset-management/adv
K2 Asset Management	03 9691 6111	k2am.com.au
Kapstream Capital	02 9234 0000	kapstream.com
L1 Capital	03 9286 7000	l1.com.au
La Trobe Financial	13 80 10	latrobefinancial.com.au
Lakehouse Capital	02 8294 9800	lakehousecapital.com.au
Lazard Asset Management	1800 825 287	lazardassetmanagement.com/au/en _ us
Lendlease	02 9236 6111	lendlease.com/au
Lennox Capital Partners	13 51 53	lennoxcapitalpartners.com.au
Lincoln	1300 676 333	lincolnindicators.com.au
Loftus Peak	02 9163 3333	loftuspeak.com.au
Loomis Sayles	+1 800 343 2029	loomissayles.com
Macquarie Investment Management	13 31 74	macquarieim.com
Magellan Asset Management	1800 6243 5526	magellangroup.com.au
Maple-Brown Abbott	02 8226 6200	maple-brownabbott.com.au
Martin Currie Investment Management	+44 131 229 5252	martincurrie.com
Mason Stevens	1300 988 878	masonstevens.com.au
Melior Investment Management	02 9004 6071	meliorim.com.au
Merlon Capital Partners	13 51 53	merloncapital.com.au
Metrics Credit Partners	1300 010 311	metricscredit.com.au
MFS International Australia	02 8228 0400	mfs.com/en-au/institutions-and-consultants.html
Milford		milfordasset.com.au
MLC Asset Management	1300 738 355	mlcam.com.au
Monash Investors		monashinvestors.com

Montaka Global Investments	02 7202 0100	montaka.com
Montgomery Investment Management	02 8223 5000	montinvest.com
Morningstar Investment Management Australia	02 9276 4550	morningstarinvestments.com.au
Munro Partners	03 9290 0900	munropartners.com.au
Mutual Limited	1300 188 802	mutualltd.com.au
Nanuk Asset Management	02 9258 1600	nanukasset.com
Natixis Investment Managers	02 8224 2900	im.natixis.com/au/home
NovaPort Capital	13 51 53	novaportcapital.com.au
OnePath Australia	133 665	onepath.com.au/home.aspx
OnePath Funds Management	02 9234 8111	onepath.com.au
Orbis Investments	1300 604 604	orbis.com/au/investor/home
Panther Trust	02 9487 8998	panthertrust.com.au
Pan-Tribal Asset Management	03 9654 3015	pantribal.com.au
Paradice Investment Management	02 8227 7400	paradice.com/au
Partners Group	02 8216 1900	partnersgroupaustralia.com.au/en
Pendal	1300 346 821	pendalgroup.com
Pengana Capital	02 8524 9900	pengana.com
Perennial	1300 730 032	perennial.net.au
Perpetual Investment Management	1800 001 575	perpetual.com.au
PIMCO	02 9279 1771	pimco.com.au/en-au
PineBridge Investments	03 8644 6800	pinebridge.com/en
Platinum Asset Management	1300 726 700	platinum.com.au
Plato Investment Management	1300 010 311	plato.com.au
PM Capital	02 8243 0888	pmcapital.com.au
Premium China Funds Management	02 9211 3888	premiumchinafunds.com.au
Prime Value Asset Management	03 9098 8088	primevalue.com.au
Principal	1800 533 1390	principalglobal.com/au
Pzena Investment Management	03 8676 0617	pzena.com
QIC	07 3360 3800	qic.com
Resolution Capital	02 8258 9188	rescap.com
Robeco	1800 780 191	robeco.com/en
Russell Investments	02 9229 5111	russellinvestments.com/au
Schroders	1300 136 471	schroders.com.au
Selector Funds Management	02 8311 7736	selectorfund.com.au
SG Hiscock	03 9612 4600	sghiscock.com.au
Smallco	02 8256 1000	smallco.com.au
Solaris Investment Management	07 3259 7600	solariswealth.com.au
Spatium Capital		spatiumcapital.com
Spheria Asset Management	1300 010 311	spheria.com.au

Spire Capital	02 9047 8800	spirecapital.com.au
State Street Global Advisors	02 9240 7600	ssga.com/au/en _ gb/individual/mf
T. Rowe Price	02 8667 5700	troweprice.com/corporate/en/home.html
Talaria Capital	1300 590 488	talariacapital.com.au
Tribeca Investment Partners	02 9640 2600	tribecaip.com
Tyndall AM	1800 251 589	tyndallam.com
UBS Asset Management (Australia)	02 9324 3222	ubs.com/au/en/asset _ management
U Ethical	1800 996 888	uethical.com
Vanguard Investments Australia	1300 655 102	vanguard.com.au
Vertium Asset Management	1800 442 129	vertium.com.au
Warakirri Asset Management	03 8613 1111	warakirri.com.au
WaveStone Capital	02 9993 9162	wavestonecapital.com.au
Western Asset Management Company	03 9016 5600	westernasset.com
Wisdom Funds	02 9099 1650	wisdomfunds.com.au
Yarra Capital Management	03 9002 1999	yarracm.com
Zurich	02 9995 1111	zurich.com.au